Times Tables Tests

Teacher's Guide

Hilary Koll and Steve Mills

Schofield&Sims

Published by **Schofield & Sims Ltd**, Dogley Mill, Fenay Bridge, Huddersfield HD8 0NQ, UK
Telephone 01484 607080
www.schofieldandsims.co.uk

First published in 2008

Authors: **Hilary Koll and Steve Mills**

British Library Cataloguing in Publication Data
A catalogue record for this book is available from the British Library.

Design by **Ledgard Jepson Ltd**
Printed in the UK by **Page Bros (Norwich) Ltd**

ISBN 978 07217 1417 2

CONTENTS

Overview

Instant recall of the times tables is essential to success in all other areas of maths. However, it is an area in which some primary school pupils struggle. **Schofield & Sims Times Tables Tests** provides rigorous and systematic practice of the times tables while supporting the broader requirements of the National Curriculum. It can be used alongside existing maths lessons or to help with homework.

Comprising two pupil books and this accompanying teacher's guide, **Times Tables Tests** is designed for pupils in Key Stage 1 and Key Stage 2. The tests in this series use a range of question types, from straightforward calculations using pictures and symbols, to one- and two-step word problems.

Although the focus is on times tables throughout, the series also covers other related topics, including doubling and halving, simple fractions and mean averages. The series is ideal for use alongside a mastery curriculum, encouraging children to make rich connections across mathematical ideas by relating multiplication facts to other areas of mathematics, such as fractions, decimals, division facts and square numbers.

Times Tables Tests and the National Curriculum

Times Tables Tests 1 and **2** and this teacher's guide match the statutory requirements for Key Stage 1 and 2 for multiplication. Though the National Curriculum requires pupils to know all of the tables up to the 12 times table by the end of Year 4, it is important to revise and reinforce the times tables throughout Years 5 and 6 to ensure that they are not forgotten. The chart below shows which pupil book is suitable for each year group.

Year	Times tables taught	Recommended pupil book
Year 2	2, 5 and 10	**Times Tables Tests 1**
Year 3	3, 4 and 8	**Times Tables Tests 1**
Year 4	6, 7, 9, 11 and 12	**Times Tables Tests 2**
Year 5	Consolidation of times tables	**Times Tables Tests 2**
Year 6	Consolidation of times tables	**Times Tables Tests 2**

Times Tables Tests 2 goes beyond the requirements of the National Curriculum by introducing the 13 times table.

Pupil book structure

Times Tables Tests 1 and **2** are both divided into two sections, with each section containing 12 one-page practice tests. The tests become gradually more challenging within each book. Each of the one-page practice tests is divided into **Parts A**, **B** and **C**. The content of the three parts differs between the two books. A sample page from each book is included on the following page to show the structure of the tests.

Times Tables Tests 1

Part A contains questions where the use of language is kept to a minimum and visual representations are used.

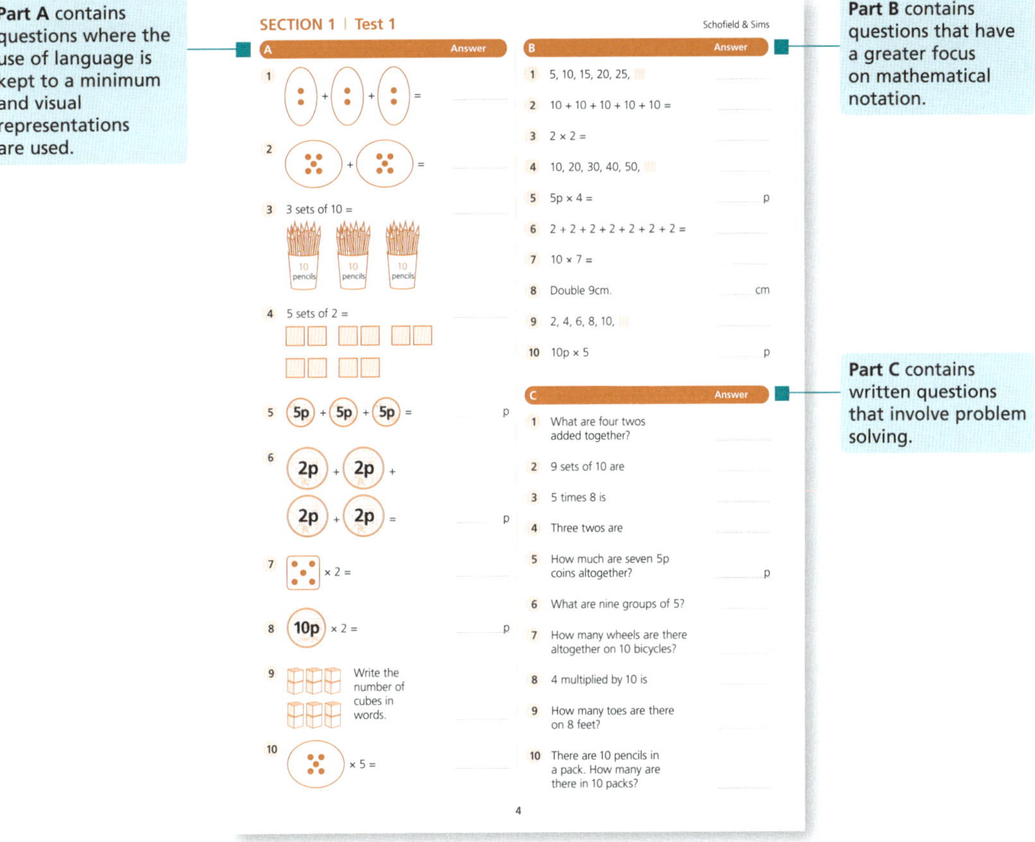

SECTION 1 | Test 1

Schofield & Sims

A Answer

1 + + =

2 + =

3 3 sets of 10 =

4 5 sets of 2 =

5 5p + 5p + 5p = p

6 2p + 2p + 2p + 2p = p

7 × 2 =

8 10p × 2 = p

9 Write the number of cubes in words.

10 × 5 =

B Answer

1 5, 10, 15, 20, 25,

2 10 + 10 + 10 + 10 + 10 =

3 2 × 2 =

4 10, 20, 30, 40, 50,

5 5p × 4 = p

6 2 + 2 + 2 + 2 + 2 + 2 + 2 =

7 10 × 7 =

8 Double 9cm. cm

9 2, 4, 6, 8, 10,

10 10p × 5 p

C Answer

1 What are four twos added together?

2 9 sets of 10 are

3 5 times 8 is

4 Three twos are

5 How much are seven 5p coins altogether? p

6 What are nine groups of 5?

7 How many wheels are there altogether on 10 bicycles?

8 4 multiplied by 10 is

9 How many toes are there on 8 feet?

10 There are 10 pencils in a pack. How many are there in 10 packs?

4

Part B contains questions that have a greater focus on mathematical notation.

Part C contains written questions that involve problem solving.

Times Tables Tests 2

Part A contains questions that use mathematical notation.

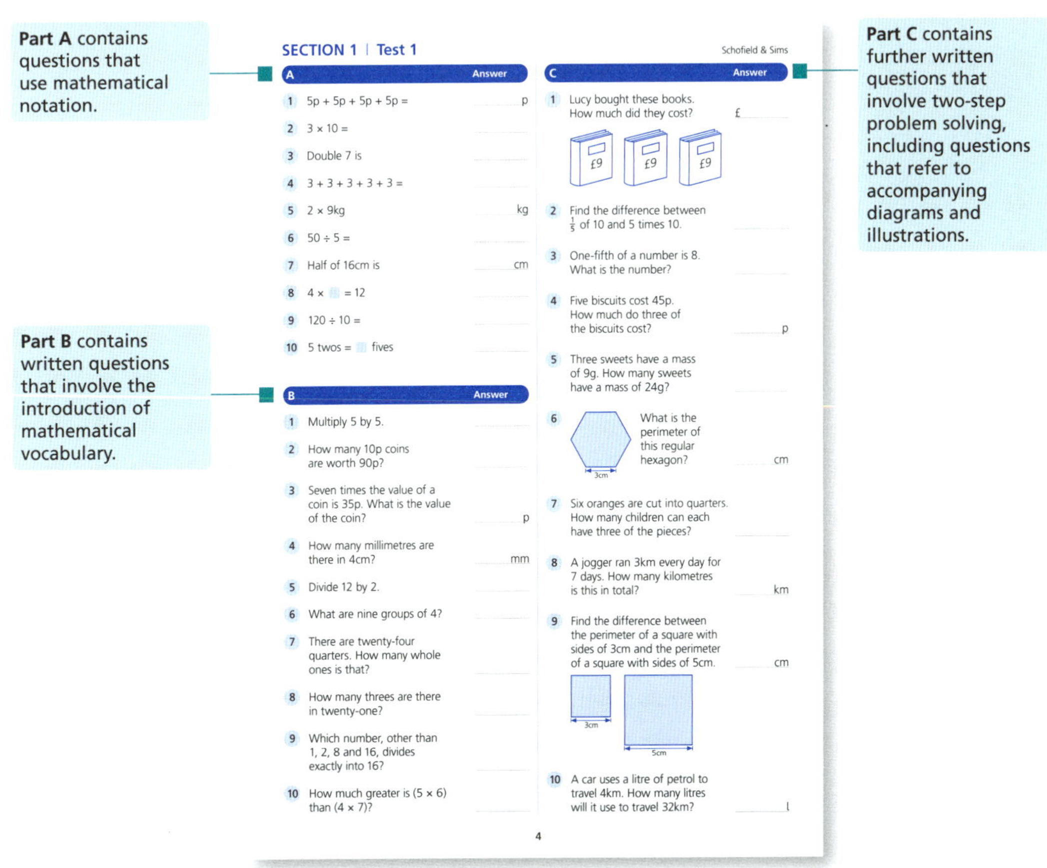

SECTION 1 | Test 1

Schofield & Sims

A Answer

1 5p + 5p + 5p + 5p = p

2 3 × 10 =

3 Double 7 is

4 3 + 3 + 3 + 3 + 3 =

5 2 × 9kg kg

6 50 ÷ 5 =

7 Half of 16cm is cm

8 4 × ☐ = 12

9 120 ÷ 10 =

10 5 twos = ☐ fives

B Answer

1 Multiply 5 by 5.

2 How many 10p coins are worth 90p?

3 Seven times the value of a coin is 35p. What is the value of the coin? p

4 How many millimetres are there in 4cm? mm

5 Divide 12 by 2.

6 What are nine groups of 4?

7 There are twenty-four quarters. How many whole ones is that?

8 How many threes are there in twenty-one?

9 Which number, other than 1, 2, 8 and 16, divides exactly into 16?

10 How much greater is (5 × 6) than (4 × 7)?

C Answer

1 Lucy bought these books. How much did they cost? £

£9 £9 £9

2 Find the difference between $\frac{1}{5}$ of 10 and 5 times 10.

3 One-fifth of a number is 8. What is the number?

4 Five biscuits cost 45p. How much do three of the biscuits cost? p

5 Three sweets have a mass of 9g. How many sweets have a mass of 24g?

6 What is the perimeter of this regular hexagon? cm

3cm

7 Six oranges are cut into quarters. How many children can each have three of the pieces?

8 A jogger ran 3km every day for 7 days. How many kilometres is this in total? km

9 Find the difference between the perimeter of a square with sides of 3cm and the perimeter of a square with sides of 5cm. cm

3cm 5cm

10 A car uses a litre of petrol to travel 4km. How many litres will it use to travel 32km? l

4

Part B contains written questions that involve the introduction of mathematical vocabulary.

Part C contains further written questions that involve two-step problem solving, including questions that refer to accompanying diagrams and illustrations.

Progress tests

Each pupil book includes two 10-minute **Progress tests**, which help you to identify gaps in understanding. The pupils should attempt each **Progress test** four times. The pupils should complete their first attempt before beginning the other tests in that section; this will give an indication of their starting level. Thereafter, the pupils complete the second attempt after they have done the first four tests in the relevant section, the third attempt after they have done the next four tests and the fourth attempt after they have done all the tests. The pupils' scores should improve with each repetition of the **Progress test**.

The pupils should time themselves when they complete a **Progress test**. Before each attempt, they should be encouraged to 'beat the clock' – without sacrificing accuracy – and improve on their previous time. This helps the pupils to approach mathematics with speed and skill, which encourages the development of mental fluency.

Each **Progress test** is accompanied by **Results charts**, which have space for the pupils to record their times and scores. Each pupil should fill out their own **Results chart** every time they attempt the test. This allows them to monitor and take pride in their progress.

Times Tables Tests Teacher's Guide

This **Times Tables Tests Teacher's Guide** contains a complete set of answers for both **Times Tables Tests 1** and **2**. The answers are presented as correctly completed pupil book pages to make marking quick and easy. There are photocopiable **Group record sheets** for keeping track of the pupils' **Progress test** scores. In addition, there are two sets of photocopiable sheets in this answer book: one for each pupil book. For **Times Tables Tests 1**, there is a photocopiable **Multiplication square**. On the square, some boxes are shaded; these indicate the times tables that the children have not yet learnt, but which have been included for fullness. Copies of this can be laminated and stuck on the pupils' desks or on a wall at home. For **Times Tables Tests 2**, there are two pages of **Multiplication facts cards** – a mixture of questions and answers. These can form the basis of practical activities; for example, you could give the pupils a selection of the cards and ask them to match the questions with the correct answers.

Using Times Tables Tests

Times Tables Tests may be used in many different ways, including:

- individual work, for pupils who are confident with the times tables
- maths recovery, to assess new or struggling pupils and to improve mental fluency
- paired work, allowing pupils who lack confidence in some concepts to discuss the questions and think of possible ways to answer them
- group or whole-class work, working through a set of questions with a group of pupils after they have answered them
- homework, where parents and carers can encourage children to work through each test with speed and, where appropriate, explain their working methods.

Administering the tests

Before administering the tests, ensure that each pupil has a sharp pencil and their pupil book open at the appropriate test.

Explain the following points to the class or pupil:

- the purpose of the test is to see which times tables the pupils know and which require more work
- they should try to do their best.

When administering the **Progress tests**, ensure that each pupil has a separate sheet of paper or a photocopy of the appropriate test. You may then distribute the tests and tell the pupils to start. Tell them to look at the classroom clock when they have finished the test and write down the time it took to complete.

Marking the tests

Use the corresponding answer pages in this book to mark the practice tests and **Progress tests**. Note the **Progress test** results on a copy of the **Group record sheet**, allowing you to track the children's progress over time. After completing the **Progress tests**, each pupil can write their own score on the **Results chart** in their pupil book.

You can mark the pupils' work yourself or you could involve the pupils in the marking process. Many teachers organise weekly whole-class marking sessions in which all the tests completed during the week are marked together. If you are teaching an individual child, this process also works on a one-to-one level. The steps for the marking sessions are as follows:

- as you prepare for the session, make sure you have the relevant answer pages to hand
- read through the test questions in turn, ensuring that everyone is focused and understands each question
- work through longer problems, modelling the most efficient method of reaching the answer
- invite one pupil to answer the question
- clearly explain to the pupils whether this answer is correct or not
- tell the pupils to mark their own answers accordingly
- if a pupil gives the wrong answer, model the correct answer on the board.

Rewarding achievement

Times Tables Tests 1 and **2** provide a permanent record of each pupil's work. The pupils are encouraged to monitor their own progress and to take pride in the development of their maths skills.

If you wish to acknowledge and reward those pupils whose achievements – at whatever level – are especially significant, you may download blank editable certificates from the Schofield & Sims website (www.schofieldandsims.co.uk/free-downloads). These certificates are also an effective way to communicate children's achievements to their parents and carers.

Strategies for learning times tables

Repetition is the key to successfully learning the times tables. It is essential, therefore, to make times tables practice a part of your everyday teaching. It is important for the pupils to master the times tables out of sequential order, so time should be dedicated to this once the basic order has been learnt. Be sure to include the various different ways of phrasing a multiplication question: 'two times seven is …', 'two multiplied by seven is …', 'two sevens are …', 'two lots of seven are …', and so on.

Though chanting the times tables individually or as a whole class is a good place to start, there are many additional strategies that will make learning the times tables easier for the pupils. By encouraging the pupils to look for patterns, learn the rule of commutativity and use a range of practical activities and games, you will set them up for success.

Looking for patterns

There is debate surrounding the best order in which to teach the times tables. However, it is generally agreed that it is best to start with 2, 5 and 10, as the patterns within them are easy for young pupils to grasp. In the 2 and 10 times tables the numbers are all even. In fact, any number multiplied by an even number will be even. In the 10 times table all the numbers end in 0 and in the 5 times table all the numbers end in 5 or 0.

Once they have mastered the 2, 5 and 10 times tables, the pupils should find it easier to move on to 4 and 8. Again, point out the patterns. Show the pupils that the answers for the 4 times table are the answers to the 2 times table doubled: for example, **3 × 4 = 3 × 2 × 2**. Likewise, the answers for the 8 times table are the answers to the 4 times table doubled: for example, **5 × 8 = 5 × 4 × 2**. Use the photocopiable **Multiplication square** to illustrate these patterns. With this foundation, the children should find it easier to move on to the rest of the times tables.

When they come to the 3, 6 and 9 times tables, the pupils will see that the digits of each answer add together to make 3, 6 or 9, or a multiple of those numbers. In the 9 times table they will also see a pattern in the tens and ones (see the first illustration in **Practical activities and games** below). There is also a trick for finding the answers in the 9 times table up to **9 × 9**. Take **6 × 9**, for example:

- To find the number for the tens column, take away 1 from the number you wish to multiply by 9: 6 – 1 = 5.
- To find the number for the ones column, use the rule that the digits of a multiple of 9 (below 90) always add up to 9. If the number in the tens column is 5, the number in the units column must be 4.
- So, **6 × 9 = 54**.

There are more tricks to learn for the higher times tables. In the 11 times table, multiples of 11 that are less than one hundred are simply the multiplied digit repeated: so **2 × 11 = 22**, **3 × 11 = 33**, **4 × 11 = 44**, and so on. Multiples of 11 that are greater than 100 also follow a pattern that, like the above pattern for the 9 times table, relies on place value. Take **12 × 11**, for example.

- First, take the number you wish to multiply by 11: **12**.
- Place its first digit in the hundreds column and its last digit in the ones column: **1_2**.
- Then add those digits together: **1 + 2 = 3**. Place that number in the tens column. This gives the correct answer of **132**.

Another useful pattern is that of the square numbers, as the numbers can be used as a framework for mastering other multiplication facts. For example, if a child needs to answer **7 × 6** and knows that **6 × 6 = 36**, they can work out the answer by adding 6 to 36.

The rule of commutativity

The rule of commutativity is useful for the pupils, because it shows that they know more than they might think. Tell the pupils that when they learn a multiplication fact, they learn three additional facts:

- When writing a multiplication, the numbers being multiplied can be written in any order. So if a pupil knows that **2 × 8 = 16**, they also know that **8 × 2 = 16**.
- For every multiplication fact there are related division facts. So if a pupil knows that **2 × 8 = 16**, they also know that **16 ÷ 2 = 8**.
- Lastly, if the pupils know that **16 ÷ 2 = 8**, they also know that **16 ÷ 8 = 2**.

As such, the rule of commutativity demonstrates to the pupils that times tables are related to other areas of maths.

Practical activities and games

It is important that written learning is supported by additional oral and practical activities. Here are some suggestions:

- Encourage the pupils to regularly write out the times tables, in addition to saying them out loud. Time the pupils while they do this and encourage them to improve on their time in each instance. When the pupils have learned all the multiplication tables, they could race each other to see who can fill out a multiplication square the fastest.
- Incorporate physical movement when reciting the times tables with the pupils. For example, when practising the 5 times table, ask the pupils to give their answers by flashing 5 fingers the appropriate number of times: so if you asked a pupil to answer **3 × 5**, they would flash 5 fingers 3 times or 3 fingers 5 times. Another useful trick is to use your fingers to demonstrate the changes in the tens and ones in the 9 times table, as the illustration on the next page demonstrates.

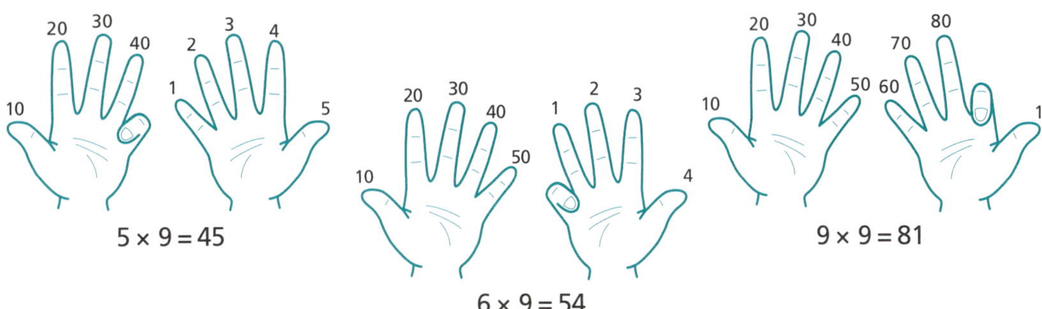

- When a pupil struggles with a particular multiplication fact, encourage them to make a flashcard with the question on one side and the answer on the other. They can take it home and stick it on their fridge or bedroom wall as a helpful reminder. Encourage parents to establish a routine in which they focus on a different multiplication fact each day.
- Ask the children to make posters, collages, displays and other artwork that illustrates what they have been learning. For example, the illustration below is a useful way of showing the variety of methods for thinking about individual multiplication facts. The pupils could make their own versions of this as a poster.

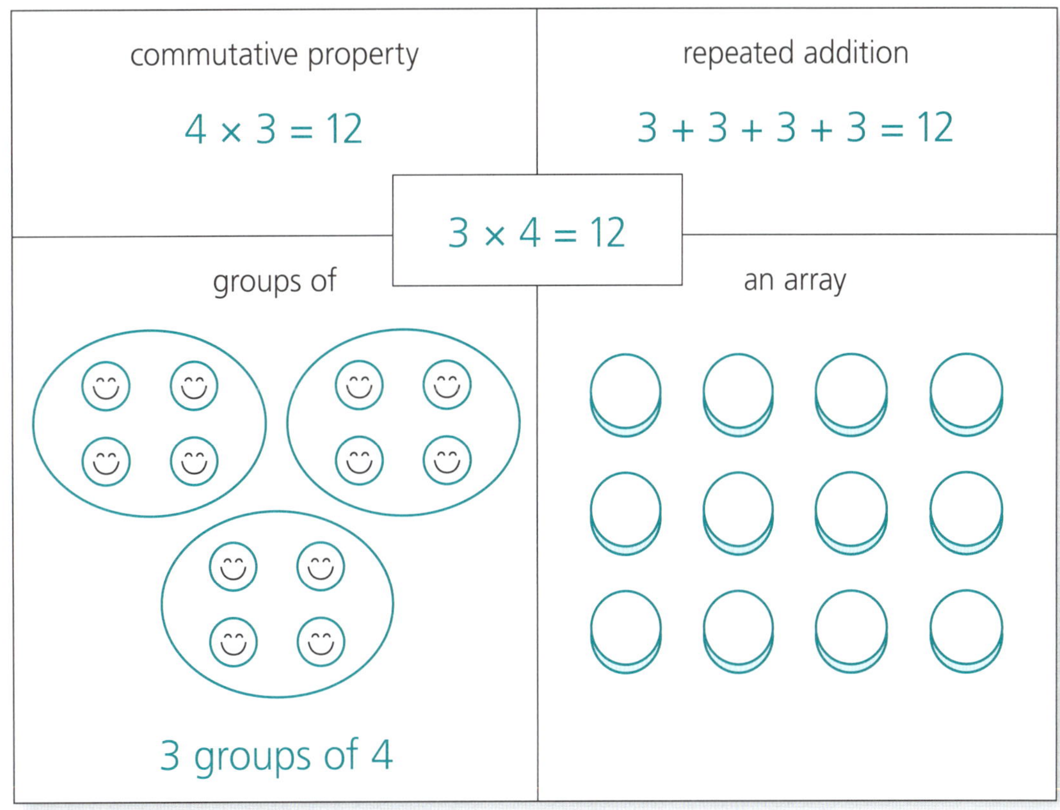

- Songs, rhymes, raps and stories can be useful tools. Encourage the pupils to make up their own.
- **The shopping game** Sit your class in a circle and say the following phrase aloud: 'I went to the shop and I bought …', followed by the first number in the times table sequence you want to practise, 'two', for example, followed by some items, 'apples', for example. The next pupil in the circle should say the same phrase, 'I went to the shop and I bought two apples', followed by 'and', the next number in the times table sequence, 'four' in this instance, and some more items, 'oranges', for example. The next pupil in the circle would then say 'I went to the shop and I bought two apples, four oranges' and then add six of another item. The pupils take turns going round the circle, repeating the items on the shopping list and adding more items according to the times table you have chosen.

- **Multiplication bingo** Give each pupil a sheet of answers to multiplication questions. Each sheet should be different. Say aloud a succession of multiplication questions. If a pupil has an answer to one of the questions on their sheet, they may cross it out. The first pupil to cross out a line of numbers on their sheet is the winner.
- **Card matching** Give each pupil a jumbled selection of matching multiplication question and answer cards. You could use the cards from the photocopiable sheets in this book or make your own. The first to match all their cards is the winner.
- **Multiple questions** Call out a number and ask the pupils to list all of the multiplication facts that have that number as the answer. For example, if you called out number 24, the pupils could give the following multiplication facts: **2 × 12**, **4 × 6**, **3 × 8**.
- **Fizz buzz** Sit the pupils in a circle. Ask them to take turns counting aloud, starting with 1. However, tell them that instead of saying some numbers, the pupils will have to say either 'fizz' or 'buzz'. Any number that is a multiple of 3 should be replaced with 'fizz' and any number that is a multiple of 5 should be replaced with 'buzz'. Therefore, the counting should go like this: 1, 2, fizz, 4, buzz, fizz, 7, 8, fizz, buzz. When a pupil comes to a number that is a multiple of both 3 and 5, such as 15, they must say 'fizz buzz'. You can increase the difficulty by introducing a third option using the word 'woof'.

Developing mental fluency

Committing the times tables to memory – and, in doing so, developing mental fluency – is vital to success in other areas of mathematics, as it frees up space in the working memory that can be dedicated to solving the rest of a mathematical problem. The times tables are the foundation of many areas of mathematics; the pupils will see this when they learn about commutativity. Times tables often feature in word problems with multiple steps, so time will be saved if they can be easily recalled.

Once the pupils are familiar with a set of times tables, test them aloud. Start in sequential order and as they get confident, mix up the questions. This process should speed up over time, until the pupils can instantly answer any question. Ensure that the pupils are confident in each multiplication set before moving on to the next one. During your regular revision time, encourage the children to write down the times tables in order, as well as reciting them aloud. Visual memory is strong and should be called upon where possible.

Daily practice is essential for developing mental fluency. Regular testing is also vital. As the practice tests in **Times Tables Tests 1** and **2** are divided into three parts, each part could be taken on a different day of the week: **Part A** on Monday, **Part B** on Wednesday and **Part C** on Friday, for example. However, the tests can be used flexibly and you should space them out according to the needs of your class or individual pupil. Doing all three parts on the same day is also fine. The repetition of the **Progress tests** is also designed to develop mathematical fluency. Retesting the pupils on the same material ensures that the knowledge is firmly embedded.

Using times tables to solve word problems

Once the pupils are able to recall multiplication facts out of sequential order, the next step is for them to apply their knowledge in different contexts. In **Times Tables Tests 1**, the pupils encounter a range of multiplication and division vocabulary, such as 'share', 'product', 'times', 'divide', 'groups of' and so on. See the glossary at the end of this book for a list of terminology. Initially, it can be useful to display these words around the classroom.

In **Times Tables Tests 2**, the pupils expand their understanding of mathematical terminology to solve more complex word problems and to apply their knowledge in increasingly difficult contexts. If a pupil struggles to solve a particular problem, encourage them to draw a simple sketch of the items involved to help them visualise it.

Times Tables Tests 1

Answers

A — Answer

1 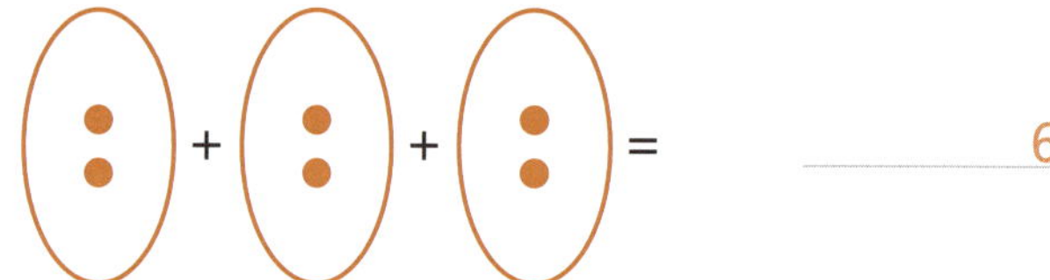 = 6

2 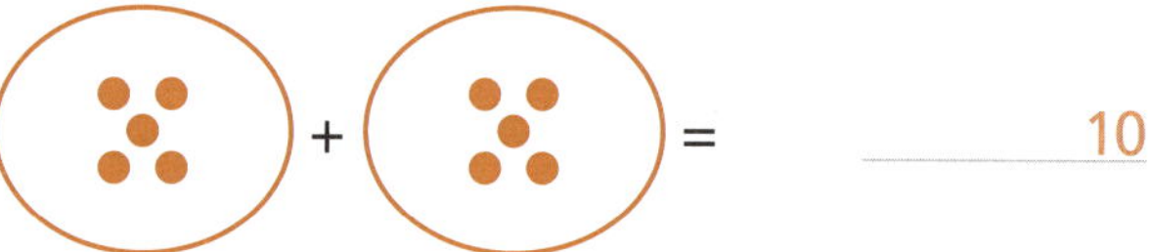 = 10

3 3 sets of 10 = 30

4 5 sets of 2 = 10

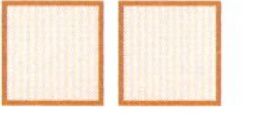 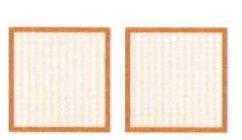 

5 5p + 5p + 5p = 15p

6 

2p + 2p + 2p + 2p = 8p

7  × 2 = 10

8 10p × 2 = 20p

9 

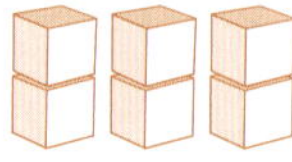

Write the number of cubes in words. twelve

10 × 5 = 25

B — Answer

1 5, 10, 15, 20, 25, ▭ 30

2 10 + 10 + 10 + 10 + 10 = 50

3 2 × 2 = 4

4 10, 20, 30, 40, 50, ▭ 60

5 5p × 4 = 20p

6 2 + 2 + 2 + 2 + 2 + 2 + 2 = 14

7 10 × 7 = 70

8 Double 9cm. 18cm

9 2, 4, 6, 8, 10, ▭ 12

10 10p × 5 50p

C — Answer

1 What are four twos added together? 8

2 9 sets of 10 are 90

3 5 times 8 is 40

4 Three twos are 6

5 How much are seven 5p coins altogether? 35p

6 What are nine groups of 5? 45

7 How many wheels are there altogether on 10 bicycles? 20

8 4 multiplied by 10 is 40

9 How many toes are there on 8 feet? 40

10 There are 10 pencils in a pack. How many are there in 10 packs? 100

A — Answer

1  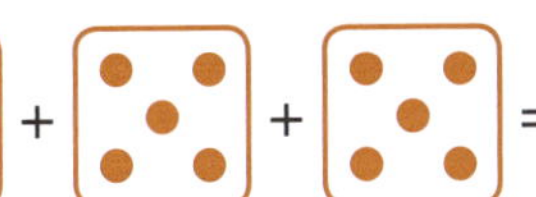 = 15

2  × 2 = 4

3    = 20p

4 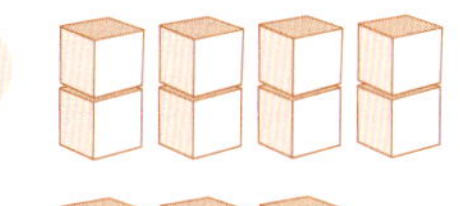 Write the number of cubes in words. fourteen

5 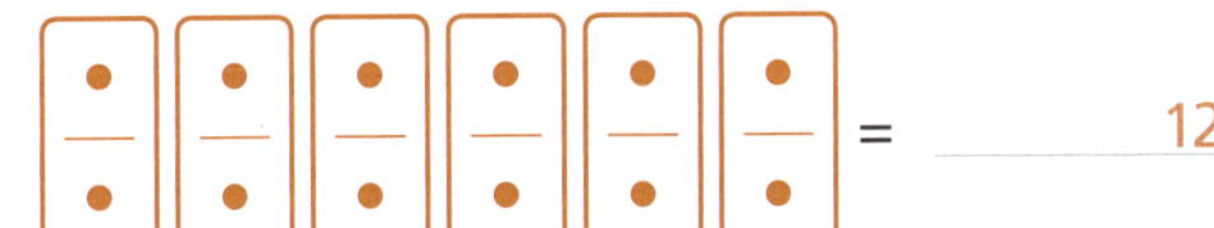 = 12

6  = 50p

7 4 sets of 10 = 40

8 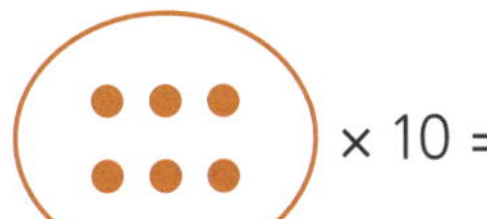 × 10 = 60

9  × 7 = 35p

10 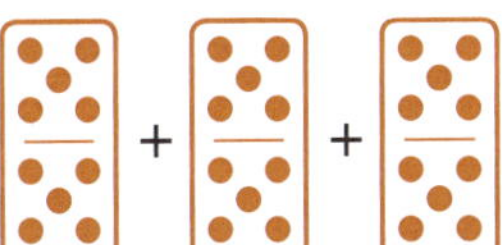 = 30

B — Answer

1 5, 10, 15, 20, ▢ 25

2 9 × 10 = 90

3 5 + 5 + 5 + 5 + 5 + 5 = 30

4 2p × 4 = 8p

5 10, ▢, 30, 40, 50 20

6 2 + 2 + 2 + 2 + 2 = 10

7 Double 9 is 18

8 8 + 8 = 16

9 2, 4, ▢, 8, 10, 12 6

10 10p × 8 = 80p

C — Answer

1 How much are nine 5p coins? 45p

2 8 sets of 5 are 40

3 7 times 10 is 70

4 Ten twos are 20

5 What are two groups of 5? 10

6 2 lots of 6 is 12

7 5 plus 5 plus 5 is 15

8 A sweet costs 5p. How much do 10 sweets cost? 50p

9 Multiply 10 by 10. 100

10 Sam is given £5 each week for 5 weeks. How much does she have now? £25

A

Answer

1 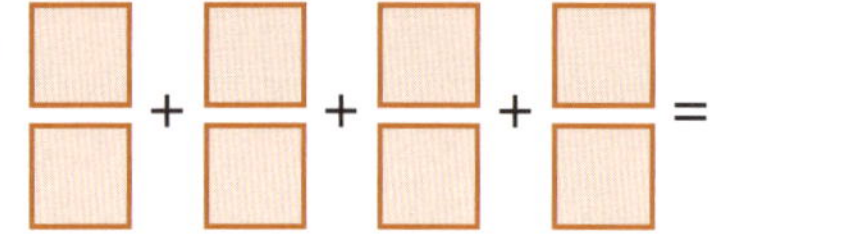 8

= 30p

3 6 sets of 2 = 12

4 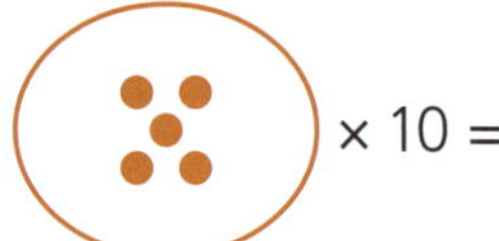 × 10 = 50

5 

= 20p

6 2 sets of 10 = 20

7 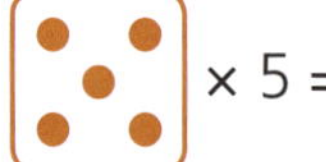 × 5 = 25

8 

× 10 = 20p

9 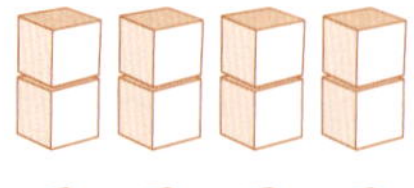 Write the number of cubes in words. sixteen

10 Count in fives to find how many. 35

B

Answer

1 10, 20, 30, 40, ▢ 50

2 5 + 5 + 5 + 5 + 5 + 5 = 30

3 Double 5 is 10

4 10p × 7 = 70p

5 2, 4, 6, 8, 10, 12, ▢ 14

6 5p × 9 = 45p

7 10 + 10 + 10 + 10 = 40

8 5 × 8 = 40

9 Twice £3 = £6

10 5, 10, ▢, 20, 25 15

C

Answer

1 Find six times ten. 60

2 When 9 is multiplied by 2 the answer is 18

3 How much are two 2p coins altogether? 4p

4 5 times 8 is 40

5 Eight tens are 80

6 What are nine sets of 10? 90

7 An apple costs 10p. How much for 6 apples? 60p

8 5 multiplied by 2 is 10

9 How many socks are there in 2 pairs? 4

10 How long is 10 lots of 10cm? 100cm

A — Answer

1   = 25p

2  = 40p

3 5 sets of 2 = 10

4 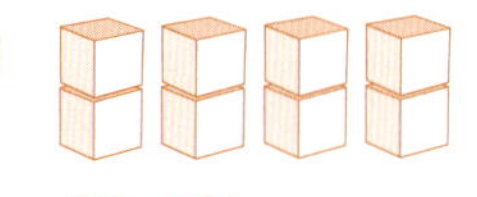 Write the number of cubes in words. twelve

5     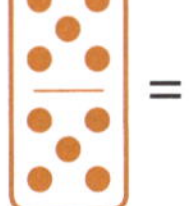 = 50

6  × 5 = 25

7 

× 3 = 30

8 Count in fives to find how many. 20

9  × 5 = 10

10 ⁞⁞ + ⁞⁞ = 8

B — Answer

1 9 + 9 = 18

2 5 × 7 = 35

3 20, 25, 30, 35, 40, ▯ 45

4 10 + 10 = 20

5 2, 4, 6, 8, 10, ▯ 12

6 5p × 8 = 40p

7 50, 60, 70, 80, 90, ▯ 100

8 2 + 2 + 2 = 6

9 5 × 3 = 15

10 Twice £8 is £16

C — Answer

1 Multiply six by ten. 60

2 Ten times two is 20

3 How much are eight 5p coins altogether? 40p

4 How many boots are there in 6 pairs? 12

5 8 times 10 is 80

6 Ten fives are 50

7 A banana costs 10p. How much for 9 bananas? 90p

8 What are seven sets of ten? 70

9 1 multiplied by 2 is 2

10 How many fingers are there on 8 gloves? 40

A — Answer

1 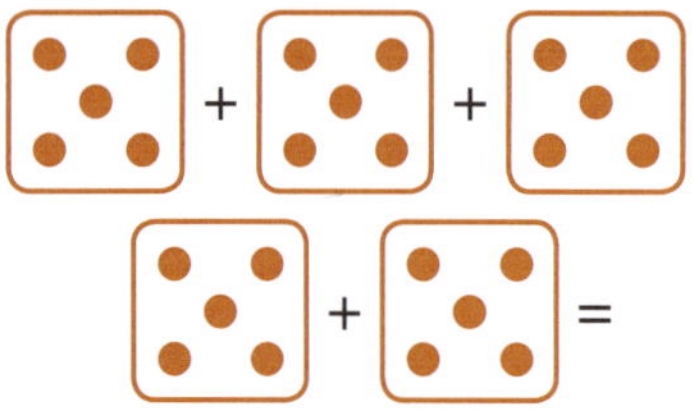 = 25

2 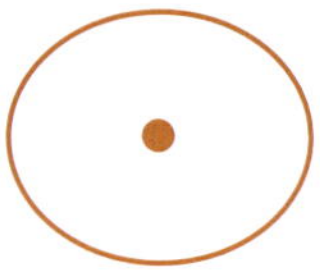 × 10 = 10

3 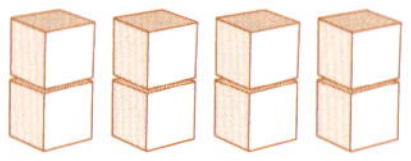 Write the number of cubes in words. eight

4 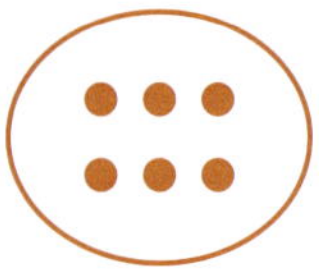 × 2 = 12

5 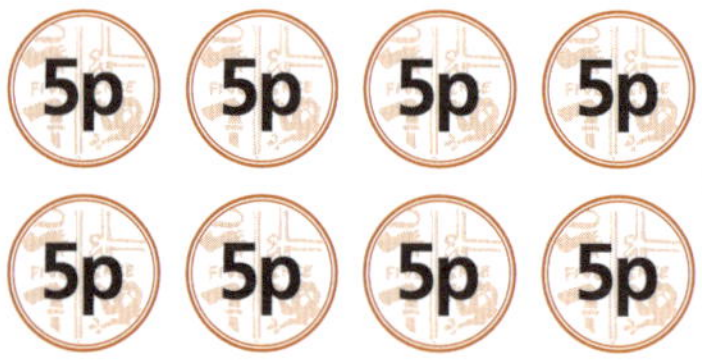

= 40p

6 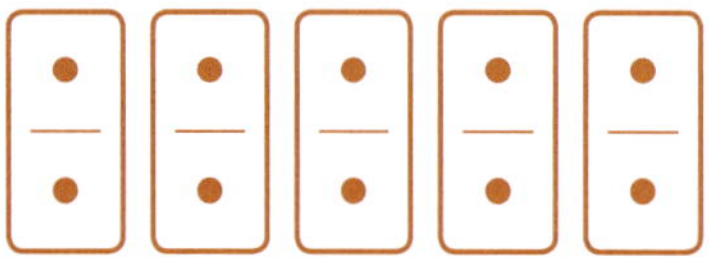 = 10

7 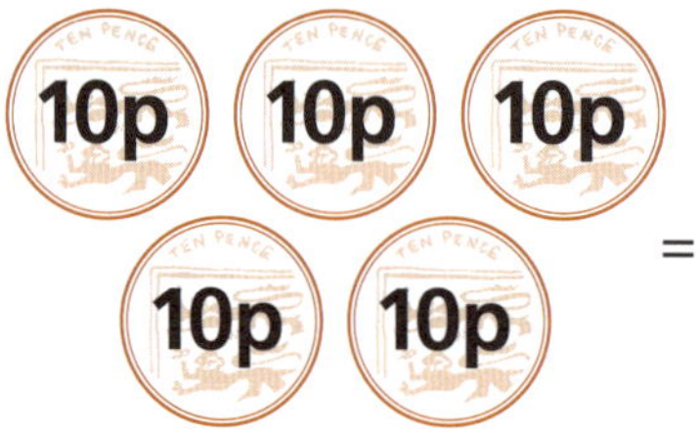

= 50p

8 4 sets of 10 = 40

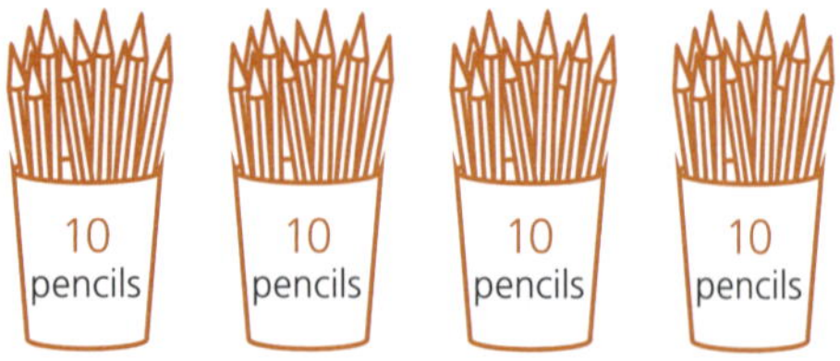

9 

× 6 = 30p

10 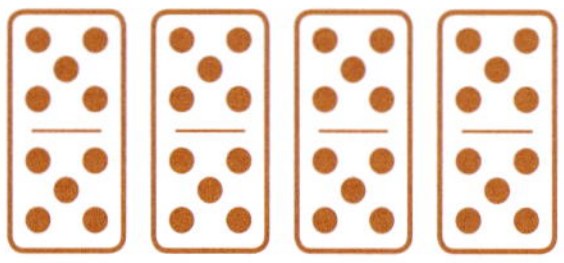 = 40

B — Answer

1 Twice 7 is 14

2 30, 35, 40, 45, ▢ 50

3 10 × 10 = 100

4 5 + 5 + 5 + 5 + 5 + 5 + 5 = 35

5 2p × 9 = 18p

6 40, 50, 60, 70, 80, ▢ 90

7 2cm + 2cm + 2cm = 6cm

8 5g + 5g + 5g = 15g

9 8, 10, 12, 14, ▢ 16

10 5p × 9 = 45p

C — Answer

1 10 plus 10 plus 10 is 30

2 2 sets of 10 are 20

3 1 times 5 is 5

4 How much are four 5p coins? 20p

5 Six tens are 60

6 Multiply 8 by 10. 80

7 Double 5 and then double the answer. 20

8 Jo earns £8 each week for 5 weeks. How much does she earn? £40

9 A toffee costs 7p. How much do 10 toffees cost? 70p

10 How many toes on 2 feet? 10

A

		Answer
1	How heavy?   5g 5g 5g	15g
2	5 sets of 10 =  10 pencils 10 pencils 10 pencils 10 pencils 10 pencils	50
3	(••••) × 10 =	40
4	5p 5p 5p 5p 5p 5p 5p =	35p
5	How many triangles? 	14
6	(dice 6) × 2 =	12
7	2p 2p 2p 2p 2p =	10p
8	Count in fives to find how many.	45
9	5p × 9 =	45p
10	(dice 3 + 3) What is the total?	6

B

		Answer
1	10cm + 10cm + 10cm =	30cm
2	Double 8 is	16
3	30, 40, 50,	60
4	5g + 5g + 5g + 5g =	20g
5	10 × 10 =	100
6	5 + 5 + 5 + 5 + 5 =	25
7	2p × 4 =	8p
8	40, 50, 60, 70,	80
9	10, 12, 14, 16,	18
10	£5 × 6 =	£30

C

		Answer
1	Two fives are	10
2	5 times 2 times 10 is	100
3	7 sets of 10 are	70
4	How much are seven 5p coins?	35p
5	1 times 2 is	2
6	Multiply 5 by 10.	50
7	Double 2 and then double the answer.	8
8	How many fingers on 6 gloves?	30
9	Oliver spends £2 each week for 10 weeks. How much does he spend?	£20
10	An orange costs 10p. How much for 4 oranges?	40p

SECTION 1 | Test 7

A

		Answer
1	⚄ + ⚄ + ⚄ + ⚄ + ⚄ =	25
2	(● ●) × 6 =	12
3	20p is how many 10ps?	2
4	14 cubes. How many sets of 2?	7

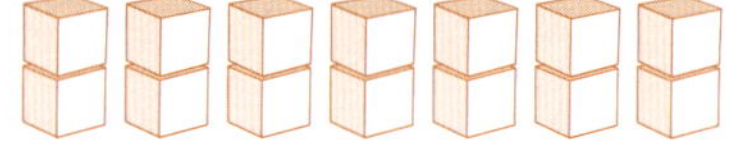

		Answer
5	shared between 10 people. How many each?	4

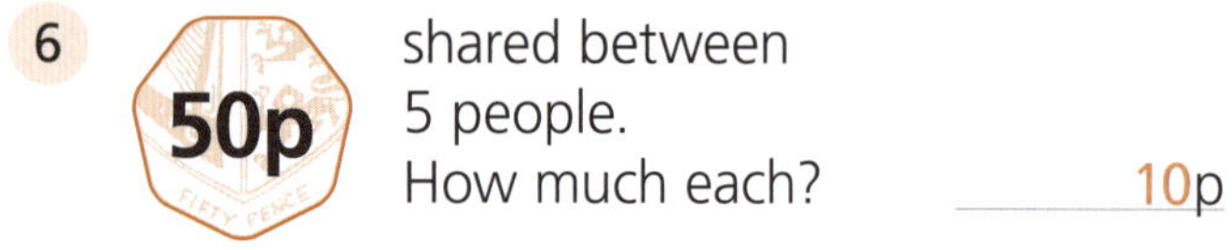

		Answer
6	50p shared between 5 people. How much each?	10p
7	÷ 2	5
8	How heavy?	6g

		Answer
9	× 10 =	90
10	5p × 9 =	45p

B

		Answer
1	8 × 10ml =	80ml
2	15 – 5 – 5 – 5 =	0
3	$\frac{1}{2}$ of 18 is	9
4	10p × 6 =	60p
5	5 + 5 =	10
6	6 × 5 =	30
7	Double 10 is	20
8	8 ÷ 2 =	4
9	25, 30, 35, 40, ☐, 50	45
10	20p ÷ 2 =	10p

C

		Answer
1	Find half of 16.	8
2	7 times 5 is	35
3	How many fives in 40?	8
4	Multiply 3 by 10.	30
5	50g shared between 5 is	10g
6	20 divided by 5 is	4
7	How many 10p coins make 100p?	10
8	A spoon holds 5 millilitres. How much do 4 spoons hold?	20ml
9	There are 18 socks. How many pairs is this?	9
10	7 tens are	70

A	Answer
1 Half of 	10p
2 10p × ☐ = 40p	4
3 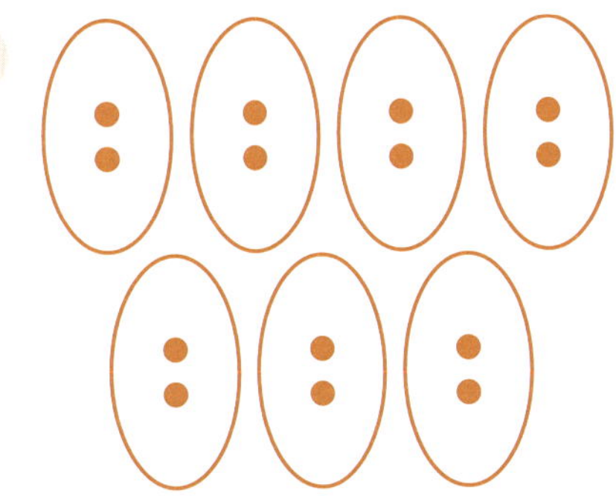	14
4  × 5 =	50
5 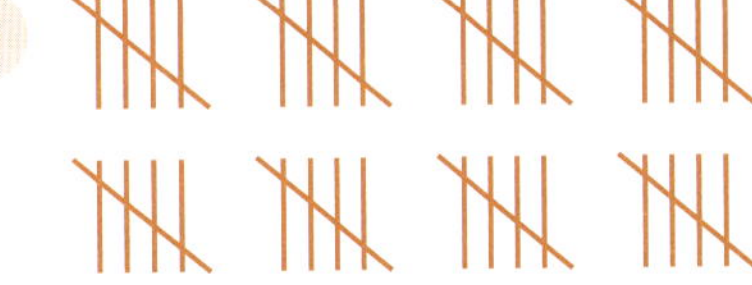	40
6 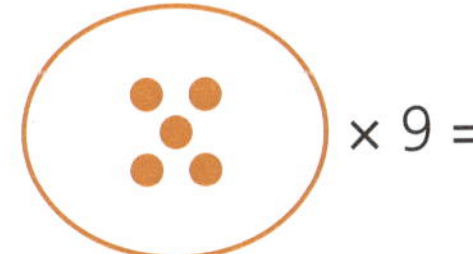 × 9 =	45
7  5p × ☐ = 20p	4
8   10 pencils 10 pencils 10 pencils ÷ 10 =	3
9  × 8 =	16
10 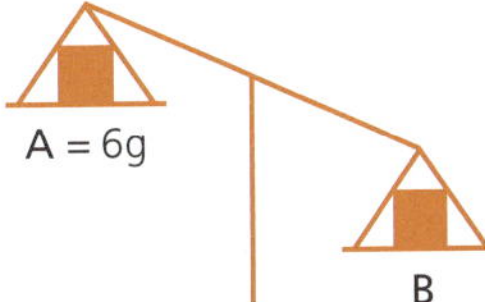 A = 6g, B. B is five times as heavy as A. How heavy is B?	30g

B	Answer
1 $\frac{1}{2}$ of 12 is	6
2 5 × 5 =	25
3 2 + 2 + 2 + 2 + 2 =	10
4 10 × 10p =	£1
5 20 – 10 – 10 =	0
6 5p × 8 =	40p
7 100, 90, 80, 70, ☐	60
8 18 ÷ 2 =	9
9 4cm + 4cm =	8cm
10 £15 ÷ 5 =	£3

C	Answer
1 Multiply seven by ten.	70
2 How many fives in 35?	7
3 Ten times eight is	80
4 90g shared between 10 is	9g
5 Forty-five divided by five is	9
6 25 divided by 5 is	5
7 £6 is shared between 2 people. How much each?	£3
8 4 multiplied by 10 is	40
9 How many 5p coins make 50p?	10
10 A pear costs 10p. I spent 70p on pears. How many did I buy?	7

SECTION 1 | Test 9

A

		Answer
1	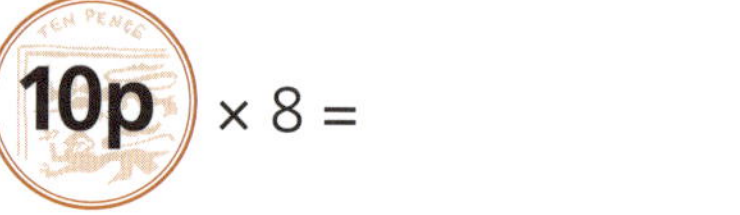 × 8 =	80p
2	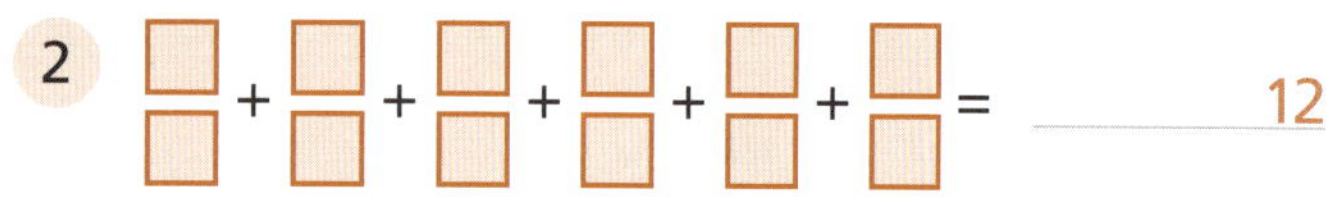	12
3	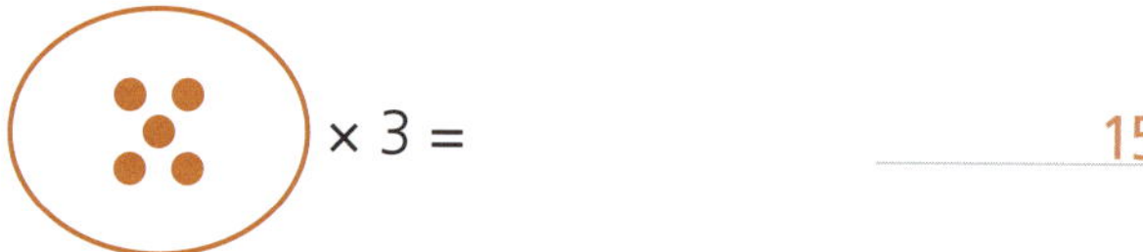 × 3 =	15
4	5p 5p 5p 5p 5p =	25p
5	 10 pencils ÷ 2 =	5
6	⚄ × 9 =	45
7	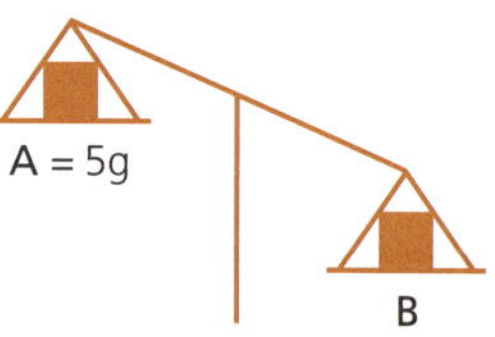 A = 5g, B. B is ten times as heavy as A. How heavy is B?	50g
8	 2p 2p 2p	6p
9	How many cubes? 	16
10	𝍸 𝍸 𝍸 𝍸 𝍸	25

B

		Answer
1	Double 10ml is	20ml
2	50, 45, 40, 35, ☐	30
3	5 + 5 + 5 + 5 + 5 =	25
4	$\frac{1}{2}$ of 18 is	9
5	90 ÷ 10 =	9
6	8 – 2 – 2 – 2 – 2 =	0
7	10p × 7 =	70p
8	20, 18, 16, ☐, 12	14
9	40 ÷ 5 =	8
10	2 × 6 =	12

C

		Answer
1	Divide 30 by 10.	3
2	How many twos in six?	3
3	5 times 10 is	50
4	How many 2p coins are equal to 20p?	10
5	What is 6 groups of 10?	60
6	There are 40 fingers. How many gloves?	8
7	There are 14 people. How many legs?	28
8	Some weights are 10g each. How heavy are 10 of these weights altogether?	100g
9	A ribbon is 50cm long. It is cut into 10 equal pieces. How long is each piece?	5cm
10	There are 8 motorbikes. How many wheels?	16

A

Answer

1. 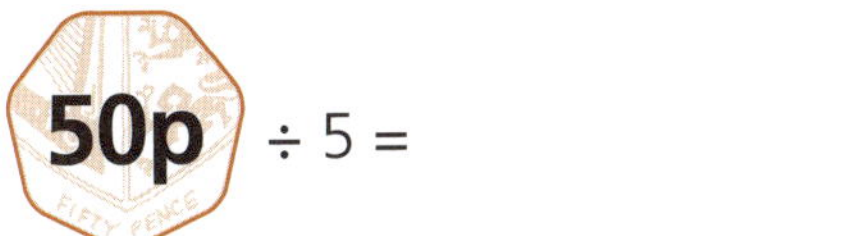 50p ÷ 5 = 10p

2. How heavy? 25g

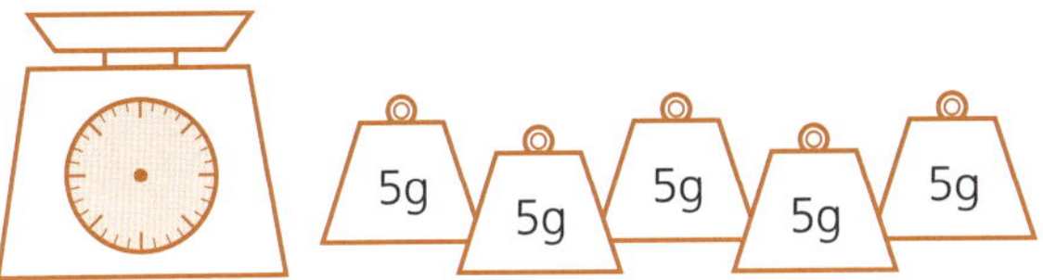

3. 3 sets of 10 = 30

4. The total weight is 16g.
How heavy is each weight?
They are both the same. 8g

5. 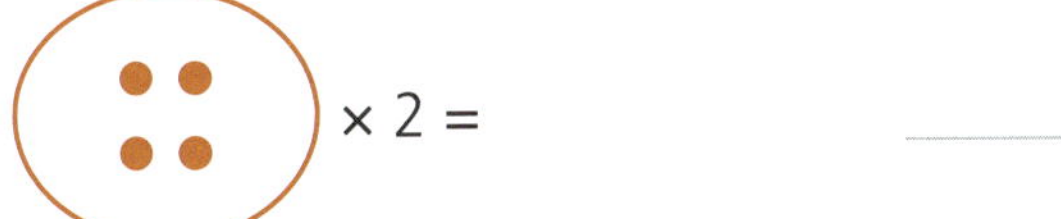 × 2 = 8

6.   

shared between 5 people.
How many each? 8

7. How many triangles? 12

8. 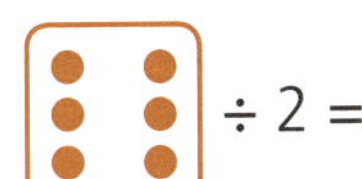 ÷ 2 = 3

9. 20p ÷ 5 =  4p

10. 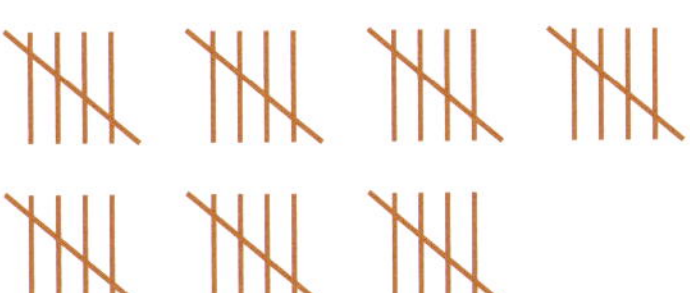 35

B

Answer

1. 20, 18, 16, ▢, 12 — 14
2. 10cm + 10cm + 10cm + 10cm = 40cm
3. Half of 18 is 9
4. 30g ÷ 5 = 6g
5. 2 × 3 = 6
6. 9 × 5ml = 45ml
7. 20 – 10 – 10 = 0
8. £40 ÷ 5 = £8
9. 100, 90, 80, ▢ — 70
10. 5 + 5 = 10

C

Answer

1. 1 times 10 is 10
2. 20 divided by 2 is 10
3. How many tens in 80? 8
4. 10 sets of 10 are 100
5. How much are three 5p coins? 15p
6. Divide 60 by 10. 6
7. Double 4 and then double the answer. 16
8. How many wheels on 7 bicycles? 14
9. Some four-legged tables have 20 legs altogether. How many tables? 5
10. Max saves £10 per week. How long before he saves £90? 9 weeks

A

		Answer
1	(2 dots) + (2 dots) + (2 dots) + (2 dots) =	8
2	7 sets of 2 =	14
3	(5 dots) × 8 =	40
4	10 pencils, 10 pencils, 10 pencils ÷ 5 =	6
5	5p × 9 =	45p
6	How many triangles?	8
7	20p ÷ 4 =	5p
8	How many sides altogether?	15
9	(5 dots) ÷ 5 =	1
10	2g × 9 =	18g

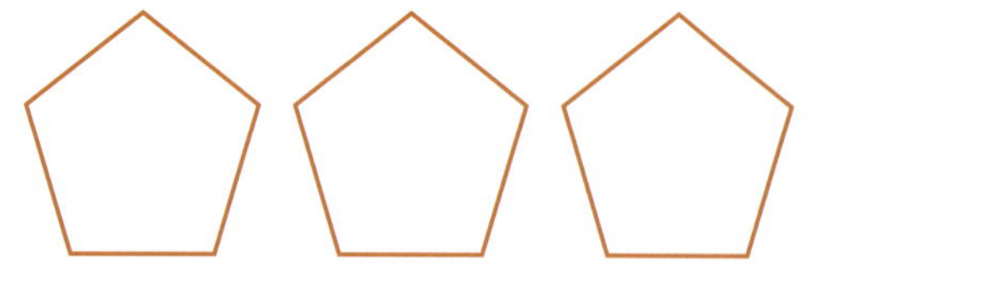

B

		Answer
1	70, 60, 50, 40, ▢	30
2	100 ÷ 10 =	10
3	8 × 2ml =	16ml
4	Halve 20.	10
5	7 + 7 + 7 + 7 + 7 =	35
6	60 ÷ 6 =	10
7	10 × 8 =	80
8	50cm ÷ 5 =	10cm
9	7 × 10 =	70
10	2 ÷ 2 =	1

C

		Answer
1	How much are three twos added together?	6
2	Divide 12 by 2.	6
3	What is half of 10?	5
4	How many fives in 25?	5
5	Four tens are	40
6	How many wheels on 3 motorbikes?	6
7	5 multiplied by 10 is	50
8	20 divided by 10 is	2
9	How many toes are there on 6 feet?	30
10	There are 10 pens in a pack. How many are there in 9 packs?	90

A — Answer

1 The total weight is 20g.
How heavy is each weight?
They are all the same. — 4g

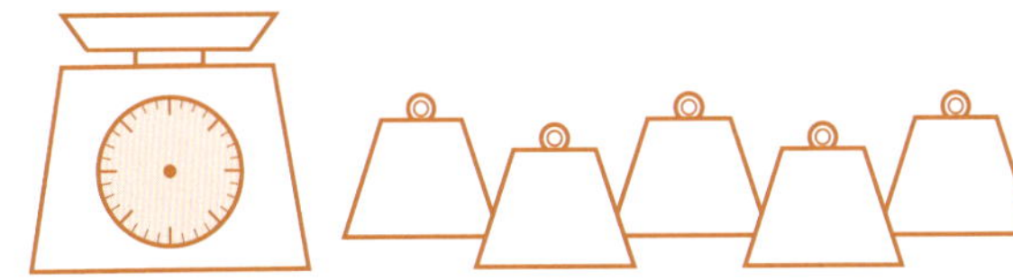

2  = — 25

3 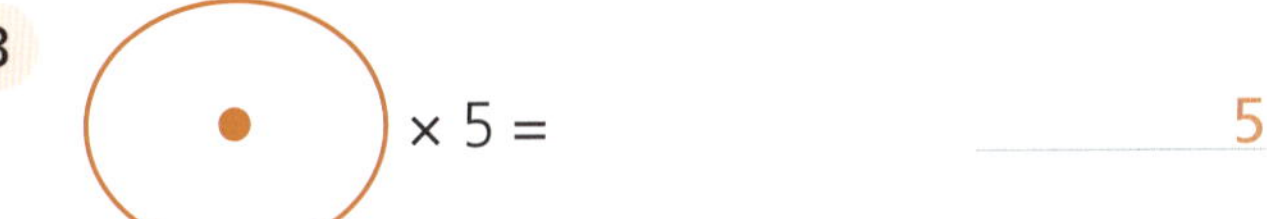 × 5 = — 5

4 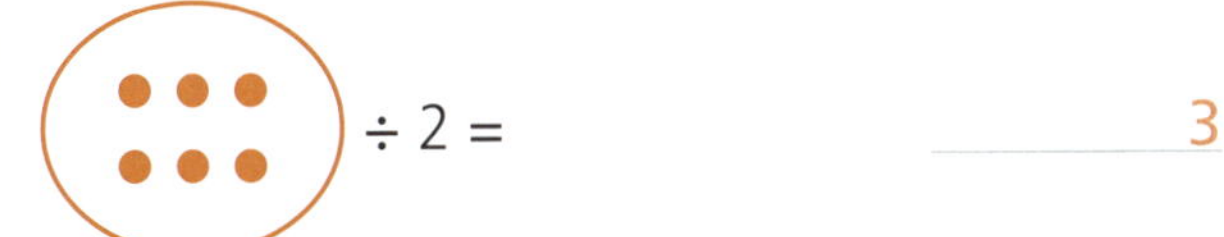 ÷ 2 = — 3

5 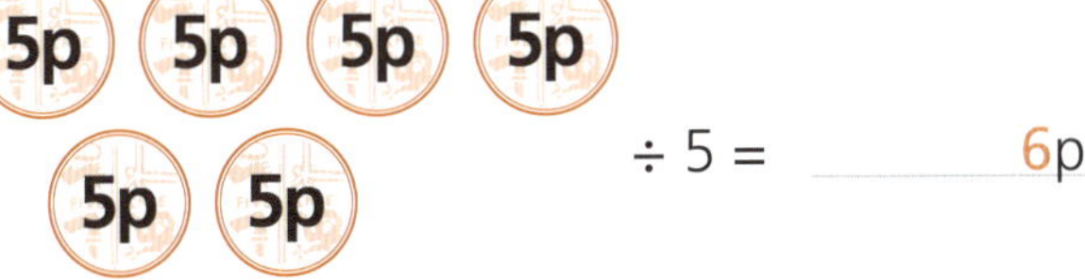

÷ 5 = — 6p

6 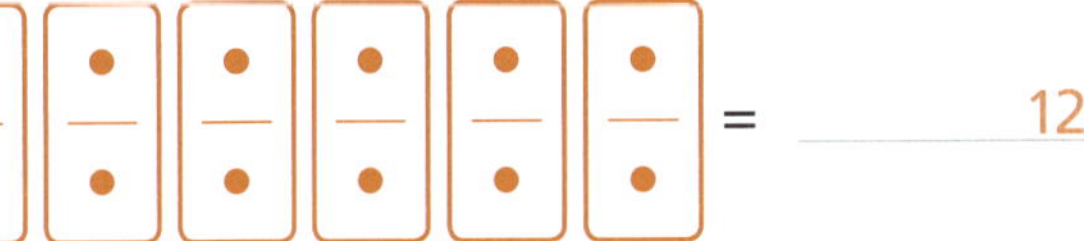 = — 12

7 

× 10 = — 100p

8 

shared between 4 = — 10

9 

× = 35p — 7

10 A = 5g, B
B is three times as heavy as A. How heavy is B? — 15g

B — Answer

		Answer
1	Double 7 is	14
2	10 – 5 – 5 =	0
3	$\frac{1}{2}$ of 16 is	8
4	2p × 7 =	14p
5	5cm + 5cm + 5cm =	15cm
6	50, 45, , 35, 30, 25	40
7	10g × 8 =	80g
8	45 ÷ 5 =	9
9	10 + 10 + 10 + 10 + 10 =	50
10	10 ÷ 2 =	5

C — Answer

		Answer
1	Seven tens are	70
2	How many groups of 2 in 20?	10
3	4 times 10 is	40
4	How many pence are ten 10p coins?	100p
5	Multiply 6 by 10.	60
6	90 divided by 9 is	10
7	Double 3 and then double the answer.	12
8	How many toes on 9 feet?	45
9	How many legs on 5 four-legged tables?	20
10	A toffee costs 5p. How much do 10 toffees cost?	50p

PROGRESS TEST 1

Write the numbers 1 to 20 down the side of a sheet of paper.
Write alongside these numbers the **answers only** to the following questions.
Work as quickly as you can. Time allowed – **10 minutes**.

1 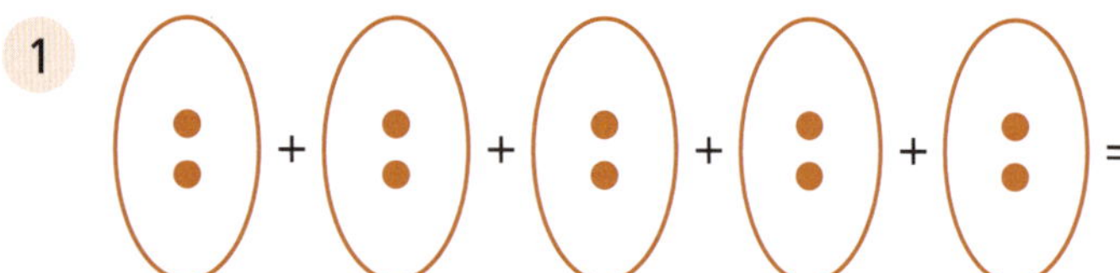 — 10

2 

10 pencils

4 sets of 10 = — 40

3 5 + 5 + 5 + 5 + 5 = — 25

4 × 2 = — 8

5 10 + 10 + 10 + 10 = — 40

6 50, 45, ___, 35, 30, 25 — 40

7 3 × 5 = — 15

8 ÷ 2 = — 3

9 Share £60 between 10 people. — £6

10 What is 6 multiplied by 2? — 12

11 What is one-half of 14m? — 7m

12 45 ÷ 5 = — 9

13 When 70 is divided by 10, what is the answer? — 7

14 What is 10 times 3? — 30

15 Double 8. — 16

16 How many 2p coins are worth the same as a 20p coin? — 10

17 A parcel weighs 4kg. How heavy are 5 parcels of the same weight? — 20kg

18 A sweet costs 5p. How much for 7 sweets? — 35p

19 What is half of 18? — 9

20 Divide 30 by 5. — 6

PROGRESS TEST 1 | Group record sheet

The **Group record sheet** can be used to record the pupils' scores each time they attempt **Progress test 1**.

Class/Set	Teacher's name

Pupil's name	1st attempt	2nd attempt	3rd attempt	4th attempt

A

		Answer
1	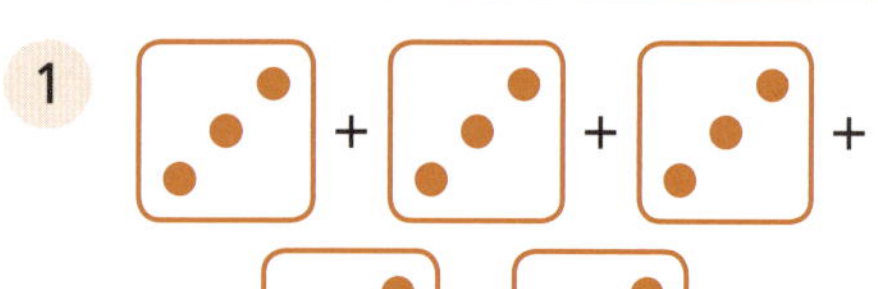 + + =	15
2	20p is how many 2ps?	10
3	(4 dots) × 2 =	8
4	+ + + =	12
5	50p ÷ 5 =	10p
6	 shared between 10 people. How many each?	5
7	× 7	70
8	3g 3g 3g	9g
9	5p × ☐ = 20p	4
10	× 5 =	45

B

		Answer
1	4, 8, 12, 16, ☐	20
2	3 × 4ml =	12ml
3	18 ÷ 3 =	6
4	1 × 4 =	4
5	$\frac{1}{2}$ of 16 =	8
6	40p ÷ 4 =	10p
7	3, 6, 9, 12, ☐	15
8	4 + 4 + 4 + 4 =	16
9	3 + 3 + 3 + 3 + 3 + 3 + 3 =	21
10	6kg ÷ 3 =	2kg

C

		Answer
1	What is four times four?	16
2	What are eight threes?	24
3	Multiply 6 by 4.	24
4	How many 5p coins make 35p?	7
5	25g shared between 5 is	5g
6	40 divided by 10 is	4
7	A spoon holds 5 millilitres. How much do 6 spoons hold?	30ml
8	There are 10 pens in a box. How many pens in 6 boxes?	60
9	What is 8 plus 8 plus 8 plus 8?	32
10	A flower has 3 petals. How many petals on 9 flowers?	27

A — Answer

1  = 12

2  × ☐ = 60p — 6

3 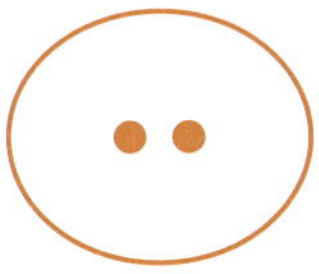 × 4 = — 8

4  ÷ 4 = — 5p

5 How many petals? — 9

6 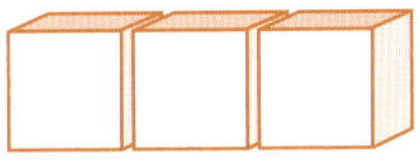 × 7 = — 21

7  = — 9

8  × 6 = — 24

9  × ☐ = 20p — 10

10 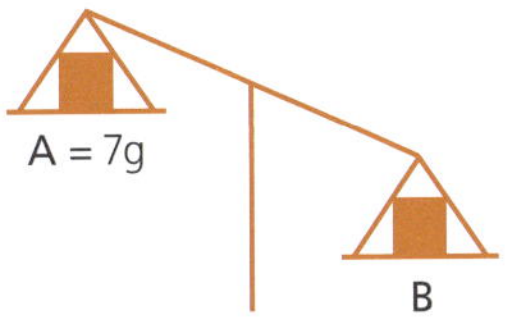

B is four times as heavy as A. How heavy is B? — 28g

B — Answer

1 8 + 8 + 8 = — 24

2 3, 6, 9, 12, ☐, 18 — 15

3 10 × 10ml = — 100ml

4 3cm + 3cm = — 6cm

5 2 × 4 = — 8

6 16 – 4 – 4 – 4 – 4 = — 0

7 8 × 2 = — 16

8 10 ÷ 10 = — 1

9 4, 8, 12, 16, ☐ — 20

10 £40 ÷ 4 = — £10

C — Answer

1 Divide 35 by 5. — 7

2 How many are six threes? — 18

3 9 multiplied by 3 is — 27

4 A sweet costs 4p. How much for 8 sweets? — 32p

5 Forty-five divided by five is — 9

6 How many fives in 25? — 5

7 How many legs are there on 9 four-legged tables? — 36

8 £6 is shared between 3 people. How much each? — £2

9 How many 5p coins make 30p? — 6

10 There are 16 shoes. How many pairs is this? — 8

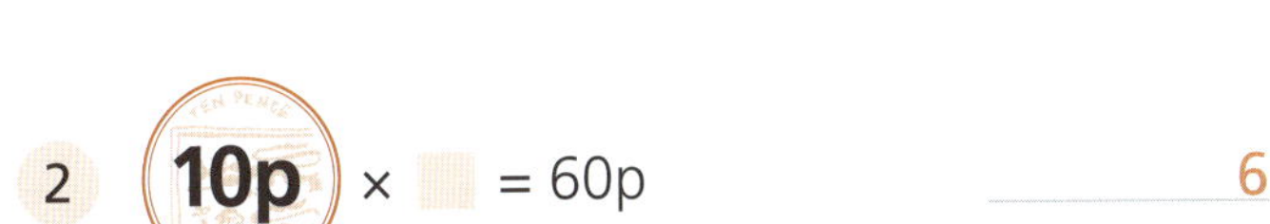

A

	Question	Answer
1	 × 10 =	£1
2	How many petals?    	15
3	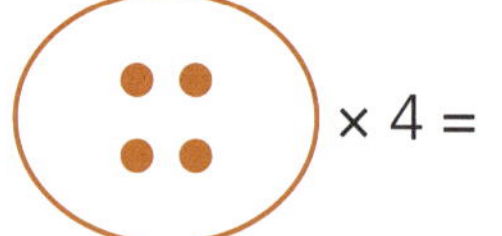 × 4 =	16
4	   =	20p
5	 ÷ 5 =	2
6	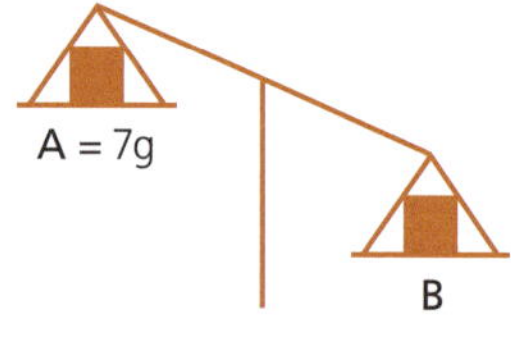 B is three times as heavy as A. How heavy is B?	21g
7	2p × 3	6p
8	The total weight is 18g. How heavy is each weight? They are all the same. 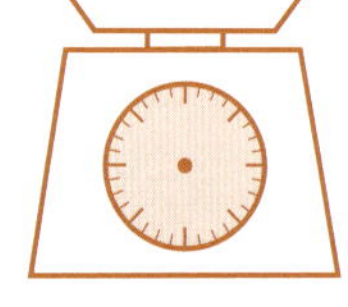 	6g
9	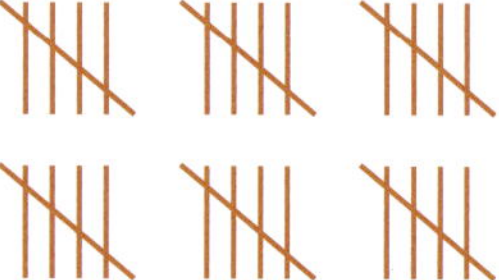	30
10	 × 6 =	24

B

	Question	Answer
1	3 × 4ml =	12ml
2	4, 8, 12, 16, ▒	20
3	8 + 8 + 8 =	24
4	£30 ÷ 3 =	£10
5	9 + 9 + 9 =	27
6	15 – 5 – 5 – 5 =	0
7	10p × 4 =	40p
8	7 + 7 + 7 + 7 =	28
9	3, 6, 9, 12, 15, 18, 21, ▒	24
10	32 ÷ 4 =	8

C

	Question	Answer
1	Divide 40 by 5.	8
2	There are 9 people. How many legs?	18
3	How many 10p coins are equal to 70p?	7
4	How many are nine fours?	36
5	There are 25 toes. How many feet?	5
6	3 divided by 3 is	1
7	What is 3 sets of 4?	12
8	Some weights are 4g each. How heavy are 2 of these weights altogether?	8g
9	A ribbon is 21cm long. It is cut into 3 equal pieces. How long is each piece?	7cm
10	8kg plus 8kg plus 8kg plus 8kg is	32kg

A — Answer

1 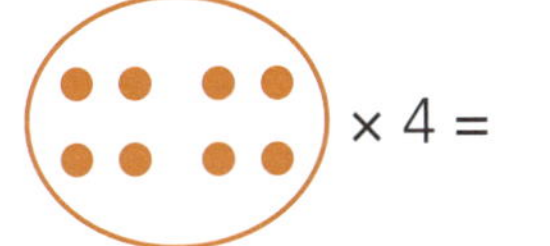 × 4 = 32

2 How heavy? 24g

3 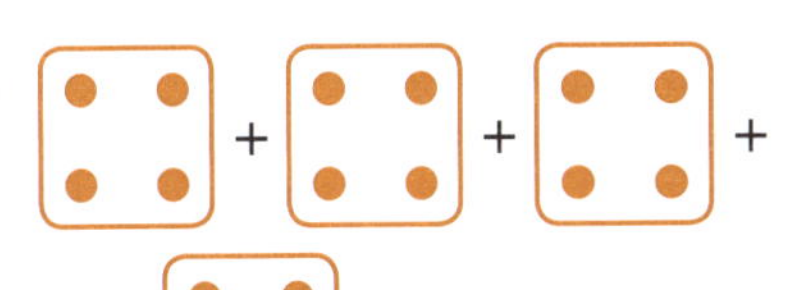 + + +

 = 16

4 5p 5p 5p 5p ÷ 4 = 5p

5 How many petals? 9

6 

shared between 3 = 10

7  × = 45p 9

8 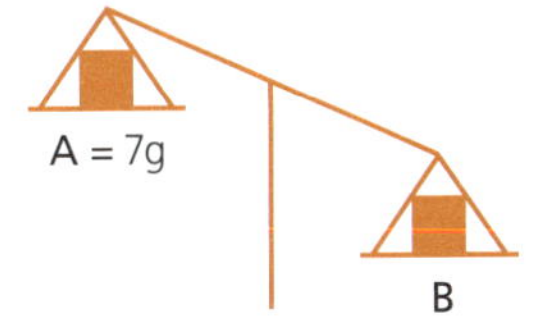

B is five times as heavy as A. How heavy is B? 35g

9 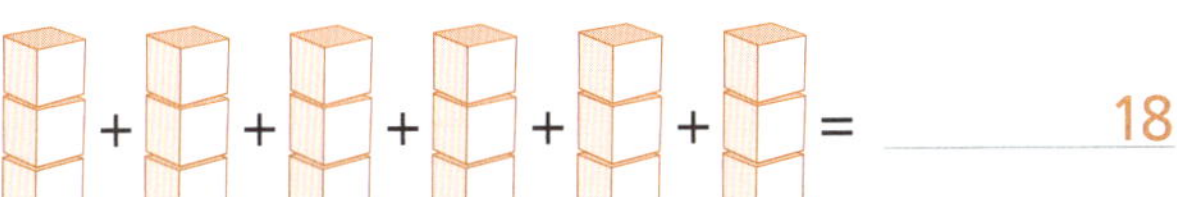 + + + + + = 18

10 How many triangles? 28

B — Answer

1 4 × 8 = 32

2 12 – 3 – 3 – 3 – 3 = 0

3 27 ÷ 3 = 9

4 4 + 4 + 4 + 4 + 4 = 20

5 2kg + 2kg + 2kg = 6kg

6 3, 6, 9, 12, ▢, 18 15

7 4g × 8 = 32g

8 20, 24, 28, 32, ▢, 40 36

9 10p + 10p + 10p + 10p = 40p

10 18 ÷ 3 = 6

C — Answer

1 Seven threes are 21

2 How many groups of 4 in 28? 7

3 8 times 3 is 24

4 How many pence are eight 5p coins? 40p

5 Multiply 3 by 8. 24

6 32 divided by 4 is 8

7 Halve 16 and then halve the answer. 4

8 How many fingers on 6 gloves? 30

9 Divide 25 by 5 and then divide the answer by 5. 1

10 A chew costs 4p. How much do 9 chews cost? 36p

A

		Answer
1	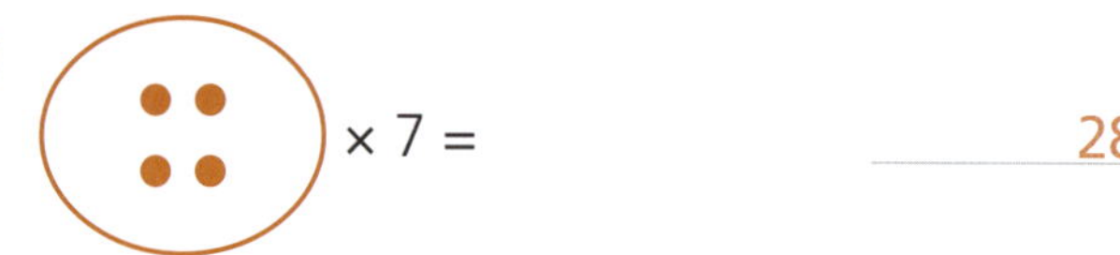 × 7 =	28
2	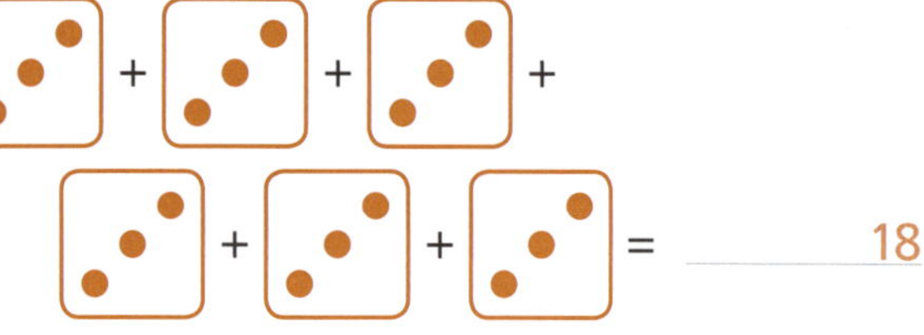 + + + + + =	18
3	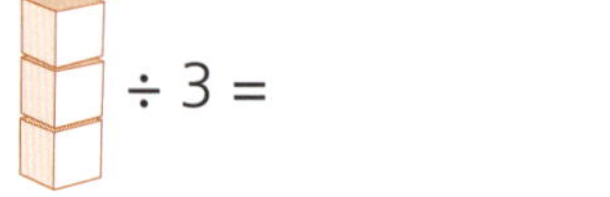 is how many lots of 4p?	5
4	 ÷ 3 =	1
5	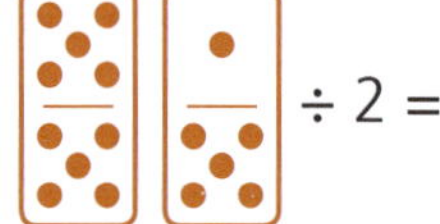 shared between 10 people. How many each?	3
6	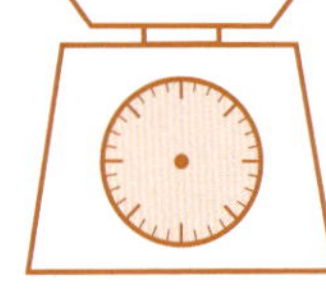 ÷ 2 =	8
7	How heavy?   	27g
8	 × ▢ = 24	4
9	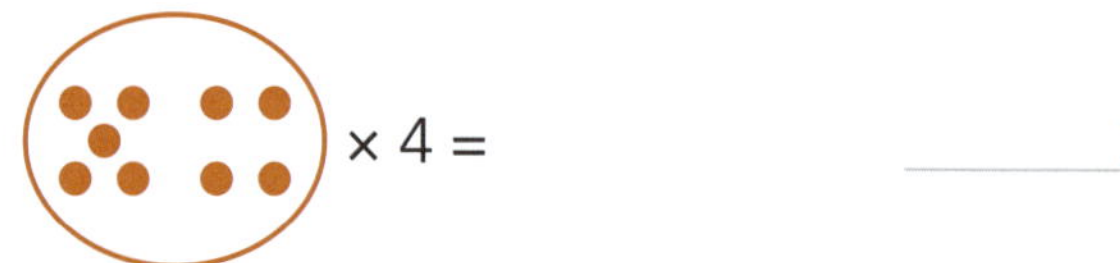 × 4 =	36
10	 You have 32p. How many 4p lollipops can you buy?	8

B

		Answer
1	3 + 3 + 3 + 3 + 3 + 3 =	18
2	30p ÷ 10 =	3p
3	4, 8, ▢, 16, 20	12
4	4 ÷ 4 =	1
5	9kg ÷ 3 =	3kg
6	3, 6, 9, 12, ▢	15
7	8 × £3 =	£24
8	3 × 7ml =	21ml
9	$\frac{1}{2}$ of 14 is	7
10	9 + 9 + 9 + 9 =	36

C

		Answer
1	What is 4 plus 4 plus 4?	12
2	What is two times four?	8
3	What are nine threes?	27
4	24 divided by 3 is	8
5	Multiply 4 by 4.	16
6	15g shared between 5 is	3g
7	A spoon holds 4 millilitres. How much do 7 spoons hold?	28ml
8	There are 4 small cakes in a box. How many cakes in 8 boxes?	32
9	How many legs are there on 7 cows?	28
10	Divide 100 by 10 and divide the answer by 5.	2

A — Answer

1.  × 8 = **32**

2. How many 3p chews could you buy? **10**

3. **14**

4. The total weight is 16g. How heavy is each weight? They are all the same. **4**g

5. 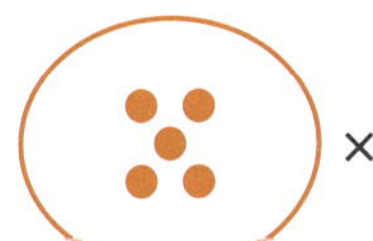 × 3 = **15**

6.   ÷ 4 = **5**p

7. How many petals? **18**

8.  × 8 = **32**

9. 

B is four times as heavy as A. How heavy is B? **24**g

10.     ÷ 4 = **9**

B — Answer

1. $\frac{1}{2}$ of 18p is **9**p
2. 16, 20, ▢, 28, 32 **24**
3. 6 + 6 + 6 = **18**
4. 8 × 5 = **40**
5. 40p ÷ 4 = **10**p
6. 12ml ÷ 3 = **4**ml
7. 9 + 9 + 9 = **27**
8. 3 × 8 = **24**
9. Twice £4 is £**8**
10. 9, 12, 15, 18, ▢ **21**

C — Answer

1. Divide 18 by 3. **6**
2. What is £24 shared between 4? £**6**
3. How much are seven 5p coins altogether? **35**p
4. ▢ groups of 4 are 28. What is the missing number? **7**
5. 27 divided by 9 is **3**
6. What are six sets of three? **18**
7. An apple costs 8p. How much for 3 apples? **24**p
8. 9 multiplied by 5 is **45**
9. How many 3p sweets can be bought with 15p? **5**
10. How many legs on 6 sheep? **24**

A — Answer

1.  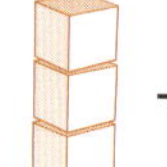 ÷ 3 = **3**

2. 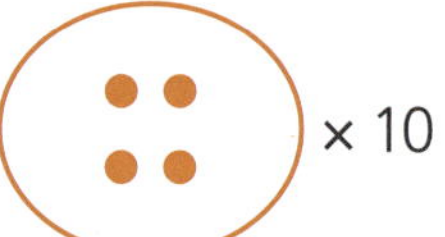 × 10 = **40**

3. 

is how many lots of 4p? **6**

4. How many? **16**
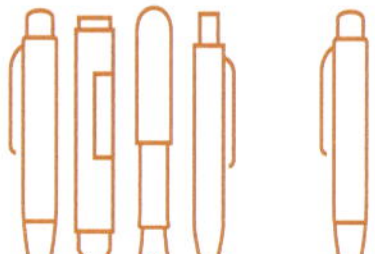 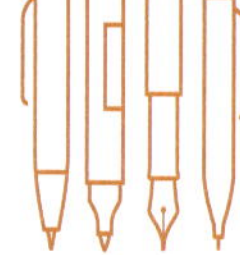

5. What is one-third of   ? **5**

6. 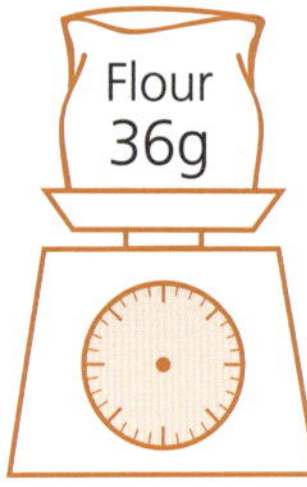

How much flour is one-quarter of this? **9g**

7.  × ☐ = 48 **8**

8. 

You have 27p. How many 3p lollipops can you buy? **9**

9.  × 8 = **24**

10. 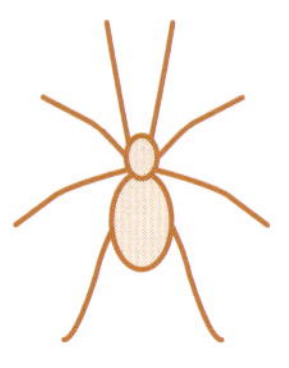 Spiders have 8 legs. How many legs do 6 spiders have? **48**

B — Answer

1. 40, 36, ☐, 28, 24, 20 **32**
2. $\frac{1}{5}$ of 25g is **5g**
3. 3 × 8ml = **24ml**
4. 8kg ÷ 4 = **2kg**
5. 8 × 8 = **64**
6. 30, 27, 24, 21, ☐ **18**
7. 1 × £3 = **£3**
8. $\frac{1}{10}$ of 70ml is **7ml**
9. 9 + 9 + 9 = **27**
10. 21 ÷ 3 = **7**

C — Answer

1. What is one-quarter of 20? **5**
2. What is three times eight? **24**
3. What are seven fours? **28**
4. £12 shared between 4 is **£3**
5. Multiply 3 by 3. **9**
6. Divide 30kg by 3. **10kg**
7. A spoon holds 4 millilitres. How many full spoonfuls can you get from 28 millilitres? **7**
8. How many 8p toffees can be bought with 24p? **3**
9. How many legs are there on 8 horses? **32**
10. How many days are there in 3 weeks? **21**

A	Answer
1 The total weight is 24kg. How heavy is each weight? They are all the same.	8kg

2 ÷ 3 =	2

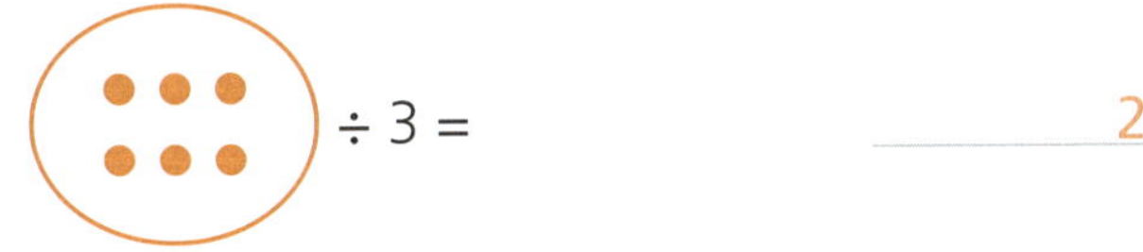

3 How much is one-quarter of this?	5p

4 =	18

5 ÷ 8 =	5p

6 × = 32	8

7 B is four times as heavy as A. How heavy is B?	32g

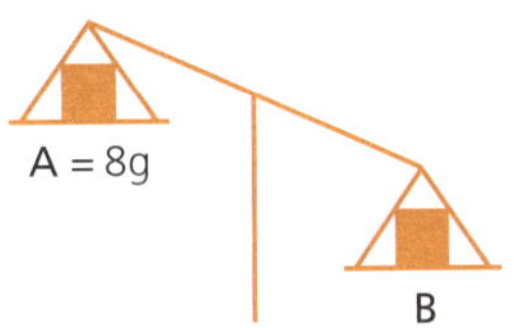

8 Find one-tenth of	5p

9 There are 72 sweets. How many groups of 8 is this?	9
10 How heavy?	27g

B	Answer
1 $\frac{1}{5}$ of 35ml is	7ml
2 16 – 4 – 4 – 4 – 4 =	0
3 40, 36, , 28, 24	32
4 7p × 4 =	28p
5 9cm + 9cm + 9cm =	27cm
6 50, 45, , 35, 30, 25	40
7 $\frac{1}{3}$ of 21g is	7g
8 40 ÷ 4 =	10
9 8 + 8 + 8 + 8 =	32
10 15 ÷ 3 =	5

C	Answer
1 Seven threes are	21
2 How many pence are ten 10p coins?	100p
3 How many groups of 3 in 12?	4
4 3 times 10 is	30
5 Divide 28 by 4.	7
6 56 divided by 8 is	7
7 How many toes on 5 feet?	25
8 What is one-third of 18kg?	6kg
9 A spoon holds 8 millilitres. How many full spoonfuls can you get from 48 millilitres?	6
10 How many 6p toffees can be bought with 54p?	9

A

		Answer
1	How heavy?	24g

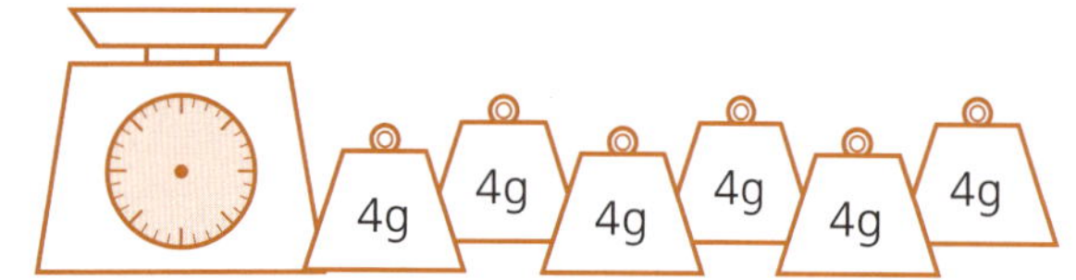

		Answer
2	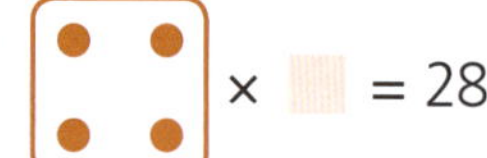 × ☐ = 28	7
3	5p × 3 =	15p
4	  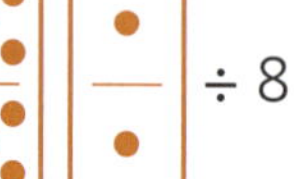 ÷ 8 =	4
5	How many petals?	24

		Answer
6	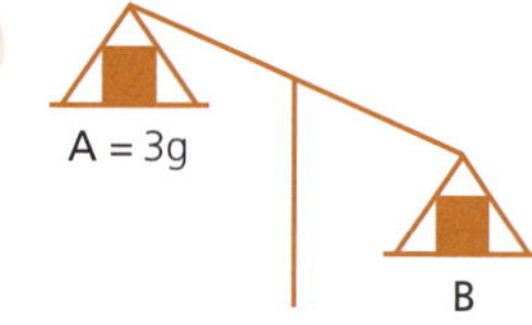 B is seven times as heavy as A. How heavy is B?	21g

		Answer
7	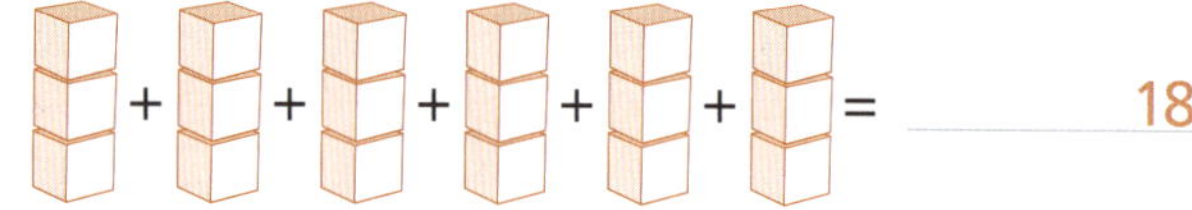	18
8	How many triangles?	20

		Answer
9	Find one-tenth of 	2p
10	There are 36 sweets. How many groups of 4?	9

B

		Answer
1	4 × 9 =	36
2	9 – 3 – 3 – 3 =	0
3	$\frac{1}{5}$ of 30g is	6g
4	24 ÷ 3 =	8
5	30, ☐, 24, 21, 18	27
6	4kg + 4kg + 4kg + 4kg =	16kg
7	$\frac{1}{3}$ of 30ml is	10ml
8	40, 36, 32, ☐, 24	28
9	10p × 10 =	£1
10	$\frac{1}{4}$ of 12 is	3

C

		Answer
1	One-third of 21 is	7
2	How many pence are nine 5p coins?	45p
3	How many groups of 4 in 40?	10
4	8 multiplied by 7 is	56
5	24 divided by 8 is	3
6	What is one-quarter of 8?	2
7	☐ groups of 3 are 18. What is the missing number?	6
8	A toffee costs 4p. How many toffees can you buy with 32p?	8
9	A 24cm ribbon is cut into 4 equal lengths. How long is each?	6cm
10	How much does it cost to buy seven 3p sweets?	21p

A — Answer

1    — 9

2 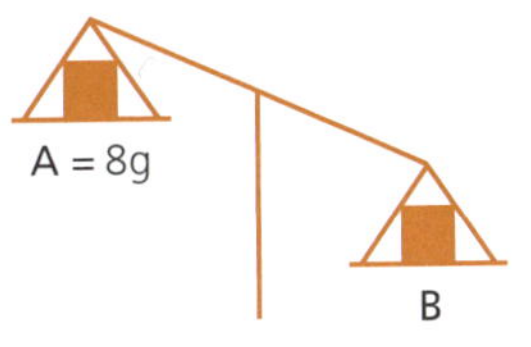

B is four times as heavy as A. How heavy is B? — 32g

3 The total weight is 36g. How heavy is each weight? They are all the same. — 6g

4  10p 2p ÷ 3 = — 4p

5 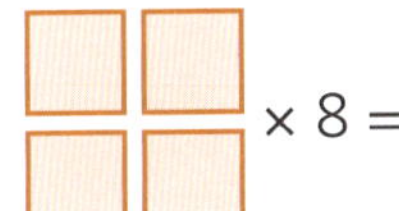 × 8 = — 32

6  × 7 — 56

7 How many petals? — 21

8  × 7 = — 28

9   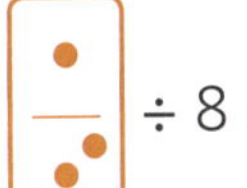 ÷ 8 = — 3

10 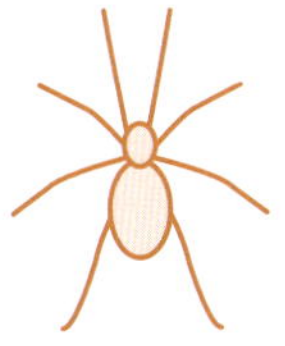 Spiders have 8 legs. How many legs do 9 spiders have? — 72

B — Answer

1 12ml ÷ 4 = — 3ml

2 $\frac{1}{3}$ of 15p is — 5p

3 72 ÷ 8 = — 9

4 36, 32, 28, 24, ☐ — 20

5 9 + 9 + 9 + 9 = — 36

6 $\frac{1}{5}$ of £25 is — £5

7 16cm ÷ 4 = — 4cm

8 9 + 9 + 9 = — 27

9 $\frac{1}{10}$ of 90 is — 9

10 18, 21, 24, ☐, 30 — 27

C — Answer

1 Divide 27 by 9. — 3

2 What is £32 shared between 8? — £4

3 ☐ groups of 5 are 45. What is the missing number? — 9

4 20 divided by 4 is — 5

5 An orange costs 7p. How much for 3 oranges? — 21p

6 How many 8p sweets can be bought with 64p? — 8

7 How much more than 20 is 8 times 3? — 4

8 Share £21 equally between 3 people. — £7

9 A number is divided by 4 and the answer is 1. What is the number? — 4

10 One-fifth of 40kg is — 8kg

A

		Answer
1	× 8 =	24
2	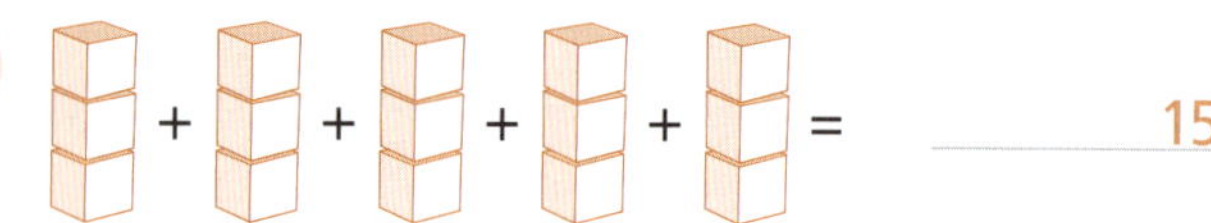	15
3	 × = 24	4
4	 ÷ 10 =	5p
5	  shared between 6 people. How many each?	5
6	 ÷ 4 =	5
7	How heavy? 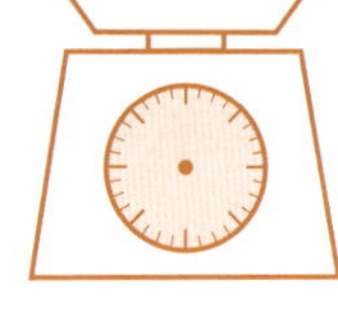 	21g
8	What is one-third of  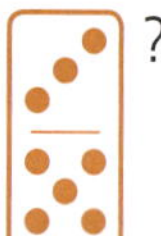 ?	6
9	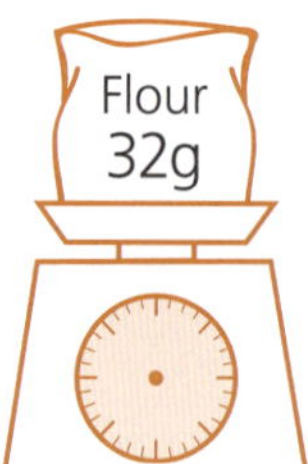 How much flour is one-quarter of this?	8g
10	 You have 56p. How many 8p lollipops can you buy?	7

B

		Answer
1	9 × 4ml =	36ml
2	27 ÷ 3 =	9
3	$\frac{1}{5}$ of 35g is	7g
4	64 ÷ 8 =	8
5	$\frac{1}{4}$ of £20 is	£5
6	35p ÷ 7 =	5p
7	18, 21, 24, 27,	30
8	12 – 4 – 4 – 4 =	0
9	4 × 8 =	32
10	3kg ÷ 3 =	1kg

C

		Answer
1	What are eight tens?	80
2	What is four times four?	16
3	One-tenth of 100 is	10
4	18g shared between 3 is	6g
5	How many eights in 24?	3
6	What is 48 divided by 8?	6
7	Eight pens fill a box. How many boxes can be filled with 32 pens?	4
8	Kim buys nine 4p chews and pays with two 20p coins. How much change does she get?	4p
9	What is one-third of 12?	4
10	A 21cm ribbon is cut into 3 equal lengths. How long is each?	7cm

A — Answer

1. 

5p ÷ 3 = — **5p**

2. How many of these make 24? — **8**

3. The total weight is 28g. How heavy is each weight? They are all the same. — **7g**

4. 
× 4 = — **16**

5.   
÷ 8 = — **3**

6. 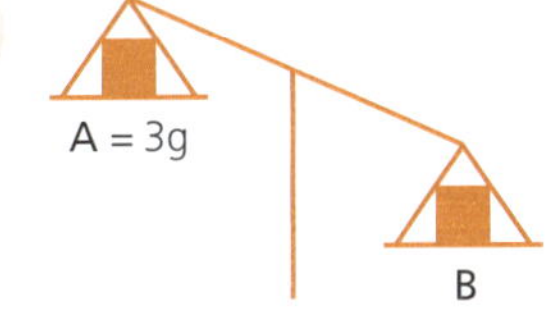

B is nine times as heavy as A. How heavy is B? — **27g**

7. 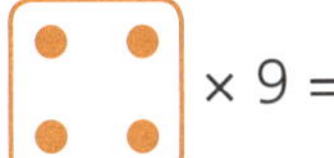
× 9 = — **36**

8. Find one-quarter of 

— **5p**

9. 
× 4 — **32**

10. 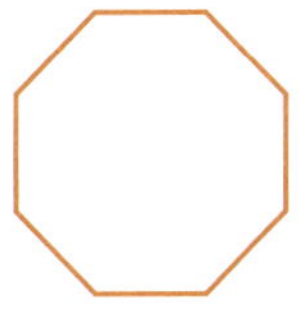
Octagons have 8 sides. How many sides have 8 octagons? — **64**

B — Answer

1. $\frac{1}{3}$ of 18ml is — **6ml**
2. 3 ÷ 3 = — **1**
3. 50, 45, 40, ▢ — **35**
4. 8 × 5 = — **40**
5. $\frac{1}{4}$ of 24 is — **6**
6. 12cm ÷ 3 = — **4cm**
7. 10 × 10 = — **100**
8. 5p × 8 = — **40p**
9. ▢, 27, 24, 21, 18 — **30**
10. 12 ÷ 4 = — **3**

C — Answer

1. Divide 40 by 4. — **10**
2. How many threes in nine? — **3**
3. How many 5p coins are equal to 45p? — **9**
4. What is 6 groups of 3? — **18**
5. Some weights are 9g each. How heavy are 3 of these weights altogether? — **27g**
6. What is one-tenth of 60? — **6**
7. A ribbon is 28cm long. It is cut into 7 equal pieces. How long is each piece? — **4cm**
8. What is 72 divided by 8? — **9**
9. Four cookies fill a box. How many boxes can be filled with 20 cookies? — **5**
10. Ana buys six 3p chews and pays with a 20p coin. How much change does she get? — **2p**

PROGRESS TEST 2

Write the numbers 1 to 20 down the side of a sheet of paper.
Write alongside these numbers the **answers only** to the following questions.
Work as quickly as you can. Time allowed – **10 minutes**.

1 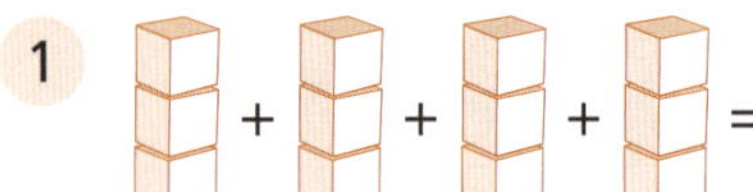 12

2 (● ● ● ●) × 2 = 8

3 4, 8, 12, 16 ▢ 20

4 3 + 3 + 3 + 3 + 3 + 3 = 18

5 4 × 4 = 16

6 (● ● ● ● ● ●) × 4 = 24

7 Divide £21 between 3 people. £7

8 What is 8 divided by 4? 2

9 $\frac{1}{5}$ of 35m is 7m

10 36 ÷ 4 = 9

11 One-tenth of 100 is 10

12 What is 9 times 3? 27

13 Multiply 8 by 8. 64

14 A parcel weighs 8kg. How heavy are 3 parcels of the same weight? 24kg

15 Eight sweets cost 48p. How much does one sweet cost? 6p

16 What is one-third of 15? 5

17 Divide 27ml by 3. 9ml

18 What is 72 divided by 8? 9

19 There are 32 sweets. How many groups of 4? 8

20 A ribbon is 24cm long. It is cut into 4 equal pieces. How long is each piece? 6cm

PROGRESS TEST 2 | Group record sheet

The **Group record sheet** can be used to record the pupils' scores each time they attempt **Progress test 2**.

Class/Set	Teacher's name

Pupil's name	1st attempt	2nd attempt	3rd attempt	4th attempt

Multiplication square

×	1	2	3	4	5	6	7	8	9	10	11	12
1	1	2	3	4	5	6	7	8	9	10	11	12
2	2	4	6	8	10	12	14	16	18	20	22	24
3	3	6	9	12	15	18	21	24	27	30	33	36
4	4	8	12	16	20	24	28	32	36	40	44	48
5	5	10	15	20	25	30	35	40	45	50	55	60
6	6	12	18	24	30	36	42	48	54	60	66	72
7	7	14	21	28	35	42	49	56	63	70	77	84
8	8	16	24	32	40	48	56	64	72	80	88	96
9	9	18	27	36	45	54	63	72	81	90	99	108
10	10	20	30	40	50	60	70	80	90	100	110	120
11	11	22	33	44	55	66	77	88	99	110	121	132
12	12	24	36	48	60	72	84	96	108	120	132	144

Times Tables Tests 2

Answers

SECTION 1 | Test 1

A

		Answer
1	5p + 5p + 5p + 5p =	20p
2	3 × 10 =	30
3	Double 7 is	14
4	3 + 3 + 3 + 3 + 3 =	15
5	2 × 9kg	18kg
6	50 ÷ 5 =	10
7	Half of 16cm is	8cm
8	4 × ☐ = 12	3
9	120 ÷ 10 =	12
10	5 twos = ☐ fives	2

B

		Answer
1	Multiply 5 by 5.	25
2	How many 10p coins are worth 90p?	9
3	Seven times the value of a coin is 35p. What is the value of the coin?	5p
4	How many millimetres are there in 4cm?	40mm
5	Divide 12 by 2.	6
6	What are nine groups of 4?	36
7	There are twenty-four quarters. How many whole ones is that?	6
8	How many threes are there in twenty-one?	7
9	Which number, other than 1, 2, 8 and 16, divides exactly into 16?	4
10	How much greater is (5 × 6) than (4 × 7)?	2

C

		Answer
1	Lucy bought these books. How much did they cost? (£9, £9, £9)	£27
2	Find the difference between $\frac{1}{5}$ of 10 and 5 times 10.	48
3	One-fifth of a number is 8. What is the number?	40
4	Five biscuits cost 45p. How much do three of the biscuits cost?	27p
5	Three sweets have a mass of 9g. How many sweets have a mass of 24g?	8
6	What is the perimeter of this regular hexagon? (3cm)	18cm
7	Six oranges are cut into quarters. How many children can each have three of the pieces?	8
8	A jogger ran 3km every day for 7 days. How many kilometres is this in total?	21km
9	Find the difference between the perimeter of a square with sides of 3cm and the perimeter of a square with sides of 5cm. (3cm, 5cm)	8cm
10	A car uses a litre of petrol to travel 4km. How many litres will it use to travel 32km?	8l

A

		Answer
1	▢ × 4 = 24	6
2	7 + 7 + 7 =	21
3	4 × 5 =	20
4	Half of 14km is	7km
5	40cm ÷ 5 =	8cm
6	$\frac{1}{3}$ of 24kg is	8kg
7	Double 9 is	18
8	2p + 2p + 2p + 2p+ 2p + 2p =	12p
9	36 ÷ 4 =	9
10	10 twos = ▢ fives	4

B

		Answer
1	How many 5p coins are equal in value to 45p?	9
2	What is one-fifth of 30?	6
3	8 plus 8 plus 8 plus 8 is	32
4	How much greater is (2 × 10) than (3 × 4)?	8
5	What is the product of 5 and 8?	40
6	Multiply (3 × 3) by 3.	27
7	How many fives are there in twenty-five?	5
8	3 times ▢ = 18	6
9	Share £28 equally between 4 boys. How much each?	£7
10	How many times smaller is 4 than 40?	10

C

		Answer
1	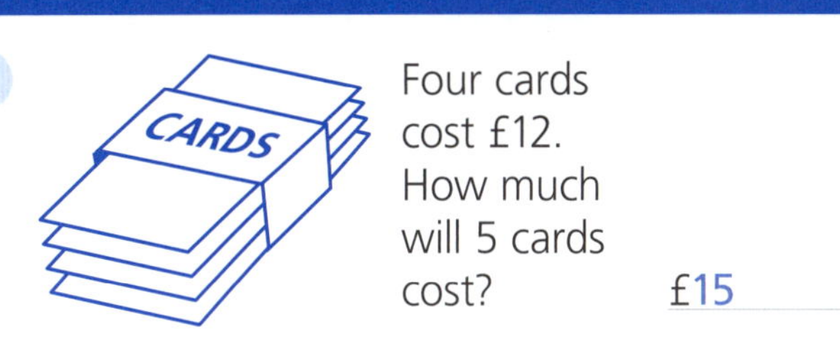 Four cards cost £12. How much will 5 cards cost?	£15
2	Write the missing number. 4 × ▢ = 2 × 8	4
3	What is zero multiplied by 7?	0
4	A bar of chocolate has 36 chunks. Saba eats $\frac{1}{4}$ of the bar. How many chunks does she eat? 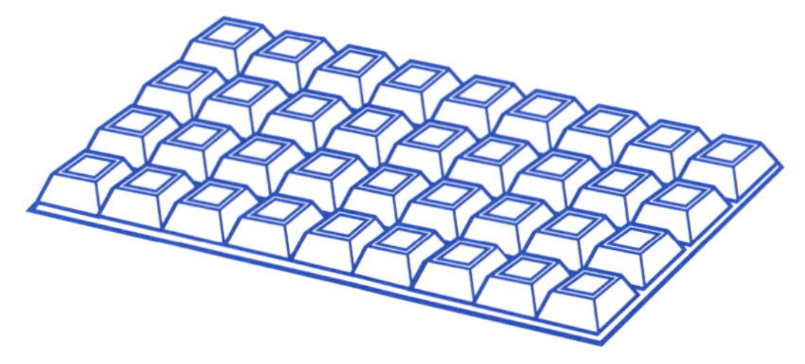	9
5	Jack saves £10 a week. How long will it take him to save £90?	9 weeks
6	A square has sides of 10cm. What is its perimeter?	40cm
7	Divide 72 by 8 and add 1.	10
8	Ron gave 3 friends 9 sweets each and he had 5 sweets left. How many did he have to start with?	32
9	A phone-call costs 5p per minute. How many minutes is a call costing 40p?	8 min
10	How many pizzas can be bought for £45 if a box of 4 pizzas costs £5?	36

SECTION 1 | Test 3

A		Answer
1	10p + 10p + 10p + 10p =	40p
2	7 × 0 =	0
3	3 × 9 = 9 + 9 + ▢	9
4	4 + 4 + 4 + 4 + 4 =	20
5	6m × 2 = 4m + 4m + ▢	4m
6	21 ÷ 3 =	7
7	Half of 18cm is	9cm
8	4 × ▢ = 28	7
9	▢ – 5 – 5 – 5 = 0	15
10	$\frac{1}{5}$ of 30kg is	6kg

B		Answer
1	How many millimetres are there in 9cm?	90mm
2	Divide 18 by 3.	6
3	What are eight groups of 4?	32
4	9kg plus 9kg plus 9kg is	27kg
5	How much greater is (5 × 5) than (1 × 10)?	15
6	What is the product of 6 and 4?	24
7	Multiply (2 × 4) by 3.	24
8	3 times 3 times 3 is	27
9	Find the difference between $\frac{1}{4}$ of 16 and $\frac{1}{2}$ of 20.	6
10	How many times larger is 45km than 5km?	9

C		Answer
1	Jim has a five-pound note. Pete has twice as much. Find the total of their money.	£15
2	● stands for a missing sign, +, –, × or ÷. 8 × 0 = 4 ● 4 What is the correct sign?	–
3	How many 5-litre cans can be filled from 40 litres of oil?	8
4	Divide the total of 29 and 6 by 5.	7
5	Find one-quarter of the product of 8 and 3.	6
6	What is the perimeter of this regular pentagon?	10cm
7	Megan has £8, Lauren has £7, Dan has £9 and Alice £12. If all their money is shared equally, how much will they each have?	£9
8	A hat costs £4. How much change from £30 would you get if you bought 7 hats?	£2
9	Find the difference between $\frac{1}{3}$ of 18 and 3 times 6.	12
10	What is zero divided by 3?	0

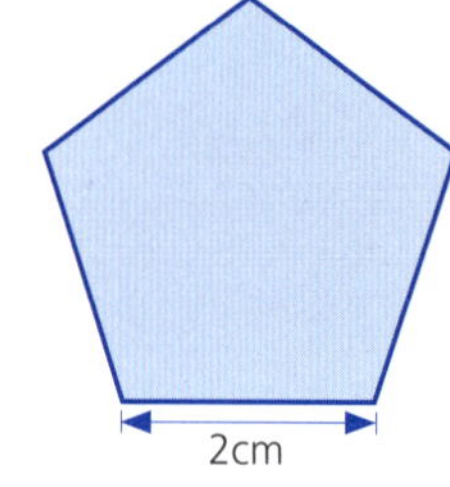

A

		Answer
1	6 × 10 =	60
2	Double 9 is	18
3	5 × ☐ = 25	5
4	2p + 2p + 2p + 2p + 2p =	10p
5	$3\overline{)24}$	8
6	4 × 7 × 0 =	0
7	20kg ÷ 5 =	4kg
8	One-quarter of 16cm is	4cm
9	10 twos = ☐ tens	2
10	14 ÷ 2 =	7

B

		Answer
1	What is one-third of 21m?	7m
2	Share £25 between 5 people.	£5
3	How many threes are there in fifteen?	5
4	4 times ☐ = 32	8
5	How many 5p coins are worth 30p?	6
6	7 plus 7 plus 7 plus 7 plus 7 is	35
7	What is the product of 3 and 6?	18
8	How many times smaller is 4 than 32?	8
9	How much greater is (3 × 10) than (6 × 4)?	6
10	Multiply (3 × 3) by 5.	45

C

		Answer
1	Three consecutive numbers, when multiplied together, give 60. What are the numbers?	3 4 5
2	Five biscuits cost 40p. How much for 2 biscuits?	16p

		Answer
3	Find the difference between $\frac{1}{4}$ of 20 and 4 times 20.	75
4	One-fifth of a number is 10. What is the number?	50
5	Four sweets have a mass of 12g. How many sweets have a mass of 27g?	9
6	Lee has nine 5p coins. Sam has one 50p coin. How much more has Sam than Lee?	5p
7	A truck uses a litre of petrol to travel 3km. How many litres will it use to travel 21 kilometres?	7l
8	Jo buys 4 kilograms of potatoes at £2 per kilogram. How much change from £10 does she get?	£2
9	The mass of a parcel is 8kg. How many times heavier is this parcel than a package weighing $\frac{1}{4}$kg?	32
10	Three oranges are cut into quarters. How many children can each have two of the pieces?	6

SECTION 1 | Test 5

A

		Answer
1	£4 + £4 + £4 + £4 =	£16
2	3 × 6 = 9 × ☐	2
3	8 + 8 + 8 =	24
4	7 × ☐ = 7	1
5	0 × 9 =	0
6	28 ÷ 4 =	7
7	Double 6cm is	12cm
8	4 × ☐ = 24	6
9	45 – 5 – 5 = ☐ × 5	7
10	$\frac{1}{10}$ of 70kg is	7kg

B

		Answer
1	Twice 8 = 4 times ☐	4
2	How many 5p coins are worth 40p?	8
3	Nine times the value of a coin is 45p. What is the value of the coin?	5p
4	How many millimetres are there in 8cm?	80mm
5	Divide 25 by 5.	5
6	What is the product of 8 and 4?	32
7	There are thirty-six quarters. How many whole ones is that?	9
8	How many threes are there in twenty-seven?	9
9	Which number, other than 1, 7 and 21, divides exactly into 21?	3
10	How much greater is (4 × 5) than (3 × 4)?	8

C

		Answer
1	A square has sides of 3cm. What is its perimeter?	12cm
2	How much greater than 50 is the answer to 8 × 8?	14
3	A packet contains 32 cookies. Ben eats $\frac{1}{4}$ of the packet. How many cookies does he eat?	8

		Answer
4	Ali saves £10 a month. How long will it take him to save enough to buy 6 mugs each costing £5?	3 mth
5	It takes an author 1 hour to write 4 pages. How long will it take her to write 24 pages?	6 hr
6	Write the missing number. 4 × ☐ = 5 × 8	10
7	Tom gave 4 friends 10 stickers each and he had 3 stickers left. How many did he have to start with?	43
8	How many apple pies can be bought for £15 if a packet of 4 pies costs £3?	20
9	Two books cost £14. How much will 5 books cost?	£35

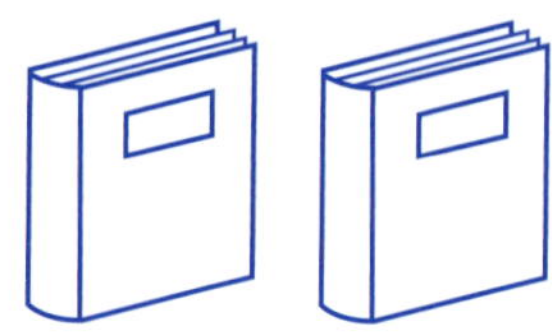

		Answer
10	Thirty-six litres of oil fill 4 identical cans. How much does each can hold?	9l

SECTION 1 | Test 6

A

		Answer
1	$\frac{1}{5}$ of 20kg is	4kg
2	£3.00 + £3.00 + £3.00 =	£9
3	3 × ▢ = 21	7
4	6 × 4 = 3 × ▢	8
5	36 ÷ 6 =	6
6	1 × 1 =	1
7	(2 × 2) × (2 × 2) =	16
8	7 × 4 =	28
9	$\frac{1}{2}$ of 18mm is	9mm
10	▢ ÷ 5 = 0	0

B

		Answer
1	What is the product of 3 and 4?	12
2	How many groups of 3 are there in 18?	6
3	3 times 3 times 5 is	45
4	What is the total mass of 5 sets of 5kg?	25kg
5	What must 4m be multiplied by to give 32m?	8
6	How many times larger is 16km than 4km?	4
7	How much greater is (5 × 9) than (3 × 5)?	30
8	Multiply (2 × 3) by 5.	30
9	Divide £40 by 5.	£8
10	What is 7 lots of 10 subtract 4 lots of 5?	50

C

		Answer
1	This line is 5cm long. Another is 7 times longer. What is its length?	35cm
2	Forty-five chairs are arranged in rows of 5. How many rows?	9
3	● stands for a missing sign, +, −, × or ÷. 7 × 10 = (7 × 5) ● 2 What is the correct sign?	×
4	What number, when multiplied by 4, will give a product of 40?	10
5	Divide the total of 9 and 7 by 4.	4
6	What is the perimeter of this hexagon?	18cm
7	Find the difference between 4 × 9 and 5 × 7.	1
8	Ella has £6, Katie has £8, Dean has £12 and David £10. If all their money is shared equally, how much will they each have?	£9
9	A t-shirt costs £4 and a pair of shorts costs £6. How much will it cost in total to buy 5 t-shirts and 3 pairs of shorts?	£38
10	What is the perimeter of an equilateral triangle with sides of 6cm?	18cm

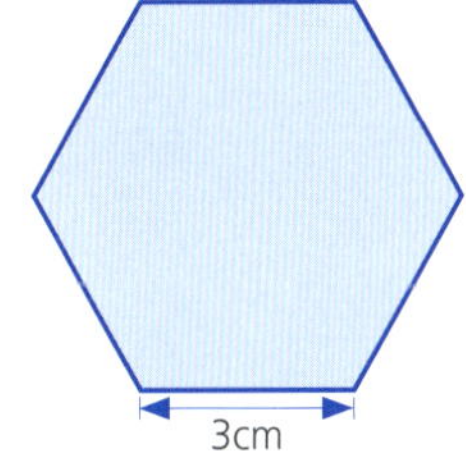

A

		Answer
1	£6 + £6 + £6 + £6 =	£24
2	7 × 7 =	49
3	Three eights are	24
4	9 + 9 + 9 + 9 + 9 + 9 =	54
5	☐ ÷ 9 = 9	81
6	32 ÷ 4 =	8
7	$\frac{1}{8}$ of 16cm is	2cm
8	7 × ☐ = 14	2
9	28kg ÷ 4	7kg
10	(4 × 2) × (3 × 2) =	48

B

		Answer
1	Share £36 equally among 6 boys. How much each?	£6
2	Find the remainder when 29 is divided by 3.	2
3	What must 5m be multiplied by to give 45m?	9
4	How many millimetres are there in 10cm?	100mm
5	Divide 72 by 9.	8
6	What is the product of 6 and 3?	18
7	How many times smaller is 4 than 36?	9
8	What are eight groups of 5?	40
9	7kg multiplied by 9 is	63kg
10	$\frac{1}{8}$ of 32 is	4

C

		Answer
1	Radu earns £6 every day doing a paper round. How much does he earn in one week?	£42
2	What is the difference between $\frac{1}{7}$ of 21 and $\frac{1}{7}$ of 35?	2
3	Six identical terraced houses are in a row. The row is 24m wide. What is the width of each house?	4m
4	A jogger travelled at the speed of 8 kilometres per hour for 15 minutes. How far did she run?	2km
5	What is the perimeter of this regular pentagon? (side 0.9cm)	4.5cm
6	Nine biscuits cost 18p. How much do five of the biscuits cost?	10p
7	Eight sweets have a mass of 56g. How many sweets have a mass of 70g?	10
8	Nine apples are cut into quarters. Six children share the pieces. How many do they each get?	6
9	A car uses a litre of petrol to travel 8km. How many litres will it use to travel 56 kilometres?	7l
10	One-eighth of a number is 10. What is the number?	80

A	Answer
1 $8 \times 8 =$	64
2 ▢ $\div 8 = 0$	0
3 $\frac{1}{9}$ of £72 is	£8
4 $36 \div 9 = 32 \div$ ▢	8
5 6×9km =	54km
6 $(8 \times 3) \div 4 =$	6
7 One-third of 18cm is	6cm
8 $7 \times$ ▢ $= 56$	8
9 ▢ $- 9 - 9 - 9 = 0$	27
10 $2 \times 3 \times 4 =$	24

B	Answer
1 How many 5p coins are equal in value to 40p?	8
2 What is one-sixth of 54?	9
3 What is 6 times 5, divided by 10?	3
4 How much greater is (5×5) than (4×4)?	9
5 What is the product of 0 and 9?	0
6 Multiply (2×3) by 7.	42
7 Twice 6 = 4 times ▢	3
8 Divide 48 by 8.	6
9 There are thirty-two quarters. How many whole ones is that?	8
10 What is the remainder when 50 is divided by 7?	1

C	Answer
1 A petrol tank, which holds 24 litres, is one-quarter full. How many more litres will it take to fill it?	18l
2 Claire gave 4 friends 7 sweets each and she had 5 sweets left. How many did she have to start with?	33
3 Three biscuits cost 27p. How much do seven of the biscuits cost?	63p
4 A square has sides of 9cm. What is the area of the square?	81cm^2
5 Six of these circular discs are placed side by side touching in a line. What is their total length?	18cm

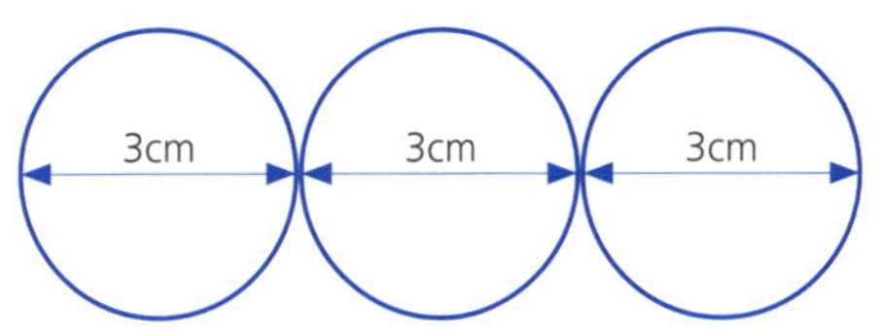

C (continued)	Answer
6 Which of these numbers can be divided by both 6 and 7 without a remainder? 12 14 18 21 24 35 42	42
7 A car uses a litre of petrol to travel 8km. How many litres will it use to travel 64 kilometres?	8l
8 Find the difference between $\frac{1}{8}$ of 56 and $\frac{1}{8}$ of 24.	4
9 Harry has a ten-pound note. William has five times as much as that. Find the total of their money.	£60
10 ● stands for a missing sign, +, −, × or ÷. $0 \times 4 = 8$ ● 8 What is the correct sign?	−

A

		Answer
1	6)48	8
2	3 × 7 =	21
3	9 fives are	45
4	4 × ☐ = £32	£8
5	9 × 6 × 2 × 0 =	0
6	7p + 7p + 7p + 7p + 7p + 7p =	42p
7	72kg ÷ 8 =	9kg
8	One-quarter of 24cm is	6cm
9	14 ÷ 2 =	7
10	30 ÷ 7 = ☐ r ☐	4 r 2

B

		Answer
1	6 plus 6 plus 6 plus 6 is	24
2	What is the product of 6 and 6?	36
3	What is one-ninth of 36m?	4m
4	Share £40 equally between 8 people.	£5
5	How many eights are there in twenty-four?	3
6	9 times ☐ = 36	4
7	How many times heavier is 54kg than 6kg?	9
8	How much smaller is (8 × 10) than (9 × 9)?	1
9	Multiply (2 × 4) by 7.	56
10	What number is equal to (9 × 7) + 7?	70

C

		Answer
1	Three notebooks cost £4.50. What will be the cost of 9 notebooks?	£13.50
2	One-eighth of a number is 8. What is the number?	64
3	Write the missing number. 4 × ☐ = 5 × 8	10
4	What is the smallest number that can be divided by both 7 and 8 without a remainder?	56
5	A bar of chocolate has 36 chunks. Josh eats $\frac{1}{6}$ of the bar. How many chunks does he eat?	6

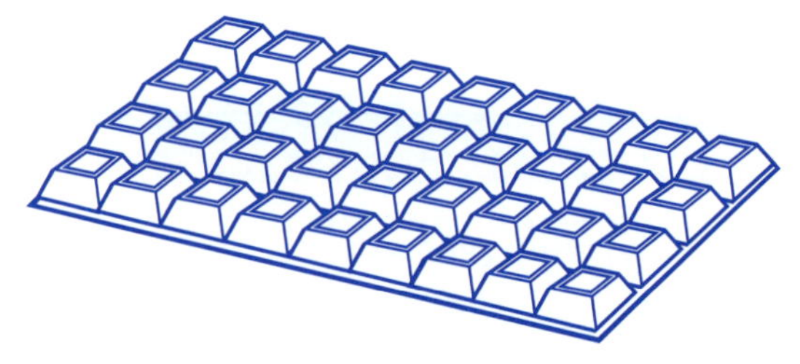

		Answer
6	What is the perimeter of an equilateral triangle with sides of 7cm?	21cm
7	A cyclist travels at 16km per hour. How far does he cycle in 15 minutes?	4km
8	Urvi has £8, Fred has £7 and Dev has £12. If all their money is shared equally, how much will they each have?	£9
9	Nine kg cost 45p. Find the price per kg.	5p
10	A square mosaic tile has an area of 7cm². Seven tiles are used to make a shape, without gaps. What is the area of the shape?	49cm²

A — Answer

		Answer
1	38 ÷ 5 = ▢ r ▢	7 r 3
2	How many days in 4 weeks?	28
3	9 + 9 + 9 + 9 + 9 =	45
4	8 × 6kg =	48kg
5	36 ÷ 4 =	9
6	$7\overline{)42}$	6
7	4 × ▢ = 16	4
8	8 × 8 =	64
9	$\frac{1}{8}$ of 24cm	3cm
10	(7 × 1) × 3 =	21

B — Answer

		Answer
1	Multiply 6 by 9.	54
2	How many 10p coins are worth 70p?	7
3	Divide 30 by 6.	5
4	What are eight groups of 7?	56
5	There are twenty quarters. How many whole ones is that?	5
6	How many centimetres is 60mm?	6cm
7	Which number, other than 1, 2, 3, 9 and 18, divides exactly into 18?	6
8	How many sixes are there in twenty-four?	4
9	How much greater is (8 × 9) than (10 × 7)?	2
10	What is one-third of 27kg?	9kg

C — Answer

1. ● stands for a missing sign, +, −, × or ÷.
   0 ÷ 6 = 3 ● 3
   What is the correct sign? **−**

2. How many 8-litre cans can be filled from 32 litres of oil? **4**

3. Abdul has a five-pound note. Sara has 8 times as much as that. Find the total of their money. **£45**

4. Divide the total of 43 and 6 by 7. **7**

5. Which of these numbers will divide into 27 without a remainder?

6	5	4	3

   3

6. The perimeter of a square is 12cm. What is its area? **$9cm^2$**

7. A shirt costs £6. How much change from £50 would you get if you bought 7 shirts? **£8**

8. What is one-quarter of the product of 6 and 6? **9**

9. What is the perimeter of this regular pentagon? **25cm**

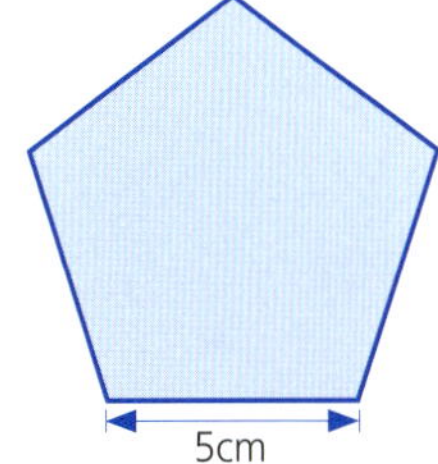

10. Find the difference between $\frac{1}{5}$ of 35 and 3 times 5. **8**

SECTION 1 | Test 11

A

		Answer
1	3×7kg =	21kg
2	$(7 \div 1) \times (6 \times 0) =$	0
3	$54 \div 6 =$	9
4	$6 \times \square = 24$	4
5	$(3 \times 2) \times \square = 48$	8
6	£8 + £8 + £8 + £8 =	£32
7	$64 \div 8 =$	8
8	$\frac{1}{9}$ of 63m is	7m
9	$\square \div 9 = 9$	81
10	$35 - 5 - 5 - 5 = \square \times 5$	4

B

		Answer
1	What is one-sixth of 30km?	5km
2	Share £49 equally between 7 people.	£7
3	How many sevens are there in fifty-six?	8
4	What number is equal to 4 times 9?	36
5	What is the product of 7 and 6?	42
6	How many times smaller is 8 than 72?	9
7	How much greater is (4×10) than (6×6)?	4
8	Multiply (2×3) by 9.	54
9	Share £28 between 7 boys. How much each?	£4
10	How many quarters in 5?	20

C

		Answer
1	When 48 is divided by a number the answer is 6. What is the number?	8
2	What is the total cost of 4 books and 3 pencil cases?	£37

		Answer
3	Elena gave 3 friends 8 sweets each and she had 7 sweets left. How many did she have to start with?	31
4	One-seventh of a number is 5. What is the number?	35
5	£18 is shared between Mo and Sash. Mo gets 5 times as much as Sash. How much does Mo get?	£15
6	Eight sweets have a mass of 56g. How many sweets have a mass of 21g?	3
7	A car uses a litre of petrol to travel 9km. How many litres will it use to travel 72 kilometres?	8l
8	A car travelled at the speed of 36km/h for 15 minutes. How many kilometres did it travel?	9km
9	This line is 4cm long. Another is 8 times longer. What is its length?	32cm
10	What is the difference between the number of days in 9 weeks and the number of minutes in one hour?	3

A		Answer
1	$\frac{1}{6}$ of 42kg is	7kg
2	1 × 1 × 1 × 1 =	1
3	9 × ☐ = 54	6
4	£9.00 + £9.00 + £9.00 =	£27
5	6 ÷ 6 = 3 ÷ ☐	3
6	49 ÷ 6 = ☐ r ☐	8 r 1
7	6 × 9 × 4 × 0 =	0
8	(3 × 3) × 7 =	63
9	$\frac{1}{8}$ of 64mm is	8mm
10	☐ ÷ 10 = 5	50

B		Answer
1	Twice 9 = 3 times ☐	6
2	Five times the value of a coin is 25p. What is the value of the coin?	5p
3	How many times less than 72 is 9?	8
4	Divide 32 by 4.	8
5	What is the product of 8 and 7?	56
6	Share the amount of money equal to nine 5p coins equally between 5 girls. How much each?	9p
7	There are thirty-six quarters. How many whole ones is that?	9
8	Which number, other than 1, 2, 8 and 16, divides exactly into 16?	4
9	By how much is $\frac{1}{7}$ of 49 greater than $\frac{1}{4}$ of 12?	4
10	How many times heavier is 42kg than 7kg?	6

C		Answer
1	Thirty-six chairs are arranged in rows of 6. How many rows?	6
2	● stands for a missing sign, +, −, × or ÷. 7 × 4 = (6 × 5) ● 2 What is the correct sign?	−
3	A t-shirt costs £3 and a pair of shorts costs £7. How much will it cost in total to buy 4 t-shirts and 3 pairs of shorts?	£33
4	What number, when multiplied by 5, will give a product of 40?	8
5	Divide the total of 18 and 6 by 4.	6
6	Matt has £20, Kieran has £5, Flynn has £10 and Mia has £1. If all their money is shared equally, how much will they each have?	£9
7	What is the area of this rectangle? 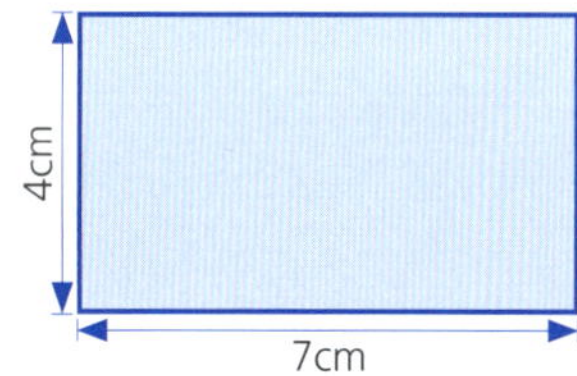	28cm^2
8	Which of these numbers will divide into 81 without a remainder? 6 7 8 9	9
9	What is the perimeter of a regular hexagon with sides of 5cm?	30cm
10	One-seventh of a number is 8. What is the number?	56

PROGRESS TEST 1

Write the numbers 1 to 20 down the side of a sheet of paper.
Write alongside these numbers the **answers only** to the following questions.
Work as quickly as you can. Time allowed – **10 minutes**.

	Question	Answer
1	$4 \times 6 =$	24
2	Share £40 equally between 8 people.	£5
3	What is the product of 3 and 7?	21
4	What is one-fifth of 30km?	6km
5	$54 \div 6 =$	9
6	When 32 is divided by a number the answer is 4. What is the number?	8
7	There are twenty-eight quarters. How many whole ones is that?	7
8	Which of these numbers can be divided by both 6 and 8 without a remainder? 18 30 36 42 48 56	48
9	The mass of a parcel is 4kg. How many times heavier is this parcel than a package weighing $\frac{1}{4}$kg?	16
10	This line is 5cm long. Another is 9 times longer. What is its length?	45cm
11	How many 7-litre cans can be filled from 35 litres of oil?	5
12	What is the remainder when 50 is divided by 7?	1
13	What is the perimeter of this regular hexagon?	42cm

	Question	Answer
14	What is the smallest number that can be divided by both 4 and 9 without a remainder?	36
15	Three biscuits cost 27p. How much do eight of the biscuits cost?	72p
16	A car uses a litre of petrol to travel 9km. How many litres will it use to travel 63 kilometres?	7l
17	A t-shirt costs £6 and a pair of shorts costs £7. How much will it cost in total to buy 6 t-shirts and 2 pairs of shorts?	£50
18	The perimeter of a square is 36cm. What is its area?	81cm²
19	A bar of chocolate has 24 chunks. Omid eats $\frac{1}{3}$ of the bar. How many chunks does he eat?	8
20	Subtract the number of days in 8 weeks from 100.	44

PROGRESS TEST 1 | Group record sheet

The **Group record sheet** can be used to record the pupils' scores each time they attempt **Progress test 1**.

Class/Set	Teacher's name

Pupil's name	1st attempt	2nd attempt	3rd attempt	4th attempt

SECTION 2 | Test 1

A

		Answer
1	30 × 8 =	240
2	6 squared is	36
3	40 + 40 + 40 + 40 =	160
4	$\frac{2}{3}$ of 9kg is	6kg
5	630 ÷ 9 =	70
6	One-quarter of 32cm is	8cm
7	6 × ☐ = 30	5
8	52 ÷ 10 = ☐ r ☐	5 r 2
9	7 × 11 =	77
10	4 tens = ☐ fives	8

B

		Answer
1	What is 9 squared?	81
2	There are twenty-one thirds. How many whole ones is that?	7
3	Find three-quarters of 36.	27
4	How many millimetres are there in 30cm?	300mm
5	Divide 280 by 4.	70
6	What are seven groups of 6?	42
7	How many eights are there in forty-eight?	6
8	What is the remainder when 57 is divided by 6?	3
9	How much smaller is (5 × 7) than (4 × 9)?	1
10	Share £720 between 9 boys. How much each?	£80

C

		Answer
1	How many weeks is equal to 49 days?	7
2	What is the difference between $\frac{1}{3}$ of 9 and 3 times 9?	24
3	One-eighth of a number is 8. What is the number?	64
4	Six biscuits cost 18p. How much do four of the biscuits cost?	12p
5	A jogger travelled at the speed of 10 kilometres per hour for 6 minutes. How many kilometres did she travel?	1km
6	A 56cm plank of wood is cut into eight pieces of equal length. What is the length of one of these pieces?	7cm
7	Find one-quarter of the product of 5 and 8.	10
8	How many half oranges can be cut from seven whole oranges?	14
9	What is the area of this rectangle?	24cm^2
10	There are seven times as many adults as children on a bus. There are 3 children. How many people on the bus?	24

A		Answer
1	$\frac{1}{4}$ of 360° is	90°
2	☐ × 5 = 15	3
3	9 + 9 + 9 + 9 + 9 + 9 + 9 =	63
4	40 × 60 =	2400
5	One-fifth of 250km is	50km
6	72cm ÷ 9 =	8cm
7	Six sixes are	36
8	4^2 =	16
9	56 ÷ ☐ = 2 × 4	7
10	55 ÷ 6 = ☐ r ☐	9 r 1

B		Answer
1	What is the remainder when 33 is divided by 8?	1
2	How many 5p coins are equal in value to 150p?	30
3	What is the product of 30 and 7?	210
4	7 plus 7 plus 7 plus 7 plus 7 plus 7 is	42
5	What is 60g multiplied by 8?	480g
6	How many sevens are there in thirty-five?	5
7	Multiply (30 × 30) by 30.	27 000
8	How much greater is 8 squared than 7 squared?	15
9	6 times ☐ = 48	8
10	Share £81 equally between 9 girls. How much each?	£9

C		Answer
1	Deepa is 4 times younger than her mother. Deepa is 7 years old. How old will her mother be in 2 years' time?	30
2	Write the missing number. 9 × 9 = 10 × 10 − ☐	19
3	What is the smallest number that can be divided by both 8 and 6 without a remainder?	24
4	Chris earns £5 a day. How many weeks will it take him to save £70?	2
5	The distance from Matby to Haw is one-third of the distance from Haw to Skern. How far is it from Matby to Skern via Haw?	32km
6	A rectangle is 9cm long and 5cm wide. What is its area?	45cm²
7	A map shows lengths 30 times smaller than in real life. How long, in real life, is a length that is 9cm on the map?	270cm
8	How long will it take to travel a distance of 180km travelling at 60km/h?	3 hr
9	How many stickers can be bought for 63p if a box of 4 stickers costs 7p?	36
10	Find one-ninth of the product of 6 and 30.	20

Skern
Haw
8km
Matby

A	Answer
1 $61 \div 9 =$ ☐ r ☐	6 r 7
2 $(8 \times 40) + (6 \times 10) =$	380
3 50p × 7 = £☐	£3.50
4 600ml × 5 =	3000ml
5 $\frac{1}{6}$ of 360° is	60°
6 $64 \div 8 = 70 -$ ☐	62
7 4 × ☐ = 44	11
8 ☐ − 7 − 7 − 7 = 0	21
9 480 minutes = ☐ hours	8
10 $\frac{2}{7}$ of 49kg is	14kg

B	Answer
1 How many minutes in 4 hours?	240
2 Divide 18 by 3 and then multiply by 9.	54
3 Multiply the sum of 6 and 2 by 4.	32
4 8kg plus 8kg plus 8kg is	24kg
5 How much greater is (6 × 7) than (4 × 9)?	6
6 What is the product of 9 and 9?	81
7 Find the square of (3 × 2).	36
8 20 times 3 times 10 is	600
9 How much greater is 4 squared than 3 squared?	7
10 How many times larger is 63km than 7km?	9

C	Answer
1 Paul has 80p. Meg has nine times as much as that. Find the total of their money.	£8
2 Forty-five pencils were put into packets of 5. How many packets were there altogether?	9
3 ● stands for a missing sign, +, −, × or ÷. 30 × 40 = 120 ● 10 What is the correct sign?	×
4 How many 500-millilitre cups can be filled from 9 litres of water?	18
5 Find the square of 7 and add 7. Then divide the total by 8.	7
6 The perimeter of this regular hexagon is 240mm. What is the length of one of its sides?	40mm
7 A badge costs £4. How much change from £30 would you get if you bought 7 badges?	£2
8 Eight parcels each have a mass of 900g. How much less than $7\frac{1}{2}$kg is their total mass?	300g
9 Find the difference between $\frac{3}{4}$ of 16 and $\frac{2}{5}$ of 20.	4
10 Which of these numbers is a multiple of 70? 45 620 49 420 100	420

A		Answer
1	7) 56	8
2	400g × 8 =	3200g
3	5 squared is	25
4	300 minutes = ☐ hours	5
5	40 ÷ 9 = ☐ r ☐	4 r 4
6	☐ ÷ 7 = 7	49
7	40 × 50 × 0 × 20 =	0
8	55 ÷ 11 =	5
9	$\frac{3}{10}$ of 90cm is	27cm
10	£1.50 ÷ 3 = ☐ p	50p

B		Answer
1	What is one-third of 27m?	9m
2	What will be the cost of 7 pencils at 60p each?	£4.20
3	What is the product of 60 and 9?	540
4	How many minutes in 6 hours?	360
5	How many threes are there in fifteen?	5
6	4 times ☐ = 48	12
7	Divide 65 by 9.	7 r 2
8	What is $\frac{3}{8}$ of 32?	12
9	How much greater is 10 squared than 9 squared?	19
10	Multiply (40 × 2) by 30.	2400

C		Answer
1	Three consecutive numbers, when multiplied together, give 210. What are the numbers?	5 6 7
2	A strip half a metre long is cut into 7-centimetre lengths. How many centimetres remain?	1cm
3	Find the cost of 5 badges if 6 badges cost 42p.	35p
4	Six pieces of wire each measure 8cm. Find the total length of the pieces in millimetres.	480mm
5	In a game Hannah scored 40 times more points than Amy. Hannah scored 800 points. How many did Amy score?	20
6	Nine sweets have a mass of 72g. How many sweets have a mass of 40g?	5
7	A van uses a litre of petrol to travel 7km. How many litres will it use to travel 280 kilometres?	40l
8	Leah buys 4 kilograms of onions at 70p per kilogram. How much change does she get from £5?	£2.20
9	The mass of a parcel is 8kg. How many times heavier is this parcel than a package weighing $\frac{1}{4}$kg?	32
10	Some tiles are 7cm wide. How many tiles can be placed side by side on this strip?	40

280cm

A

	Question	Answer
1	$3^2 + 1 =$	10
2	$80 \times 5 = 4 \times \square$	100
3	$90° + 90° + 90° =$	270°
4	$\square \div 5 = 5$	25
5	$(7 \times 30) + (4 \times 50) =$	410
6	$320 \div 40 =$	8
7	$\frac{4}{5}$ of 45kg is	36kg
8	180 minutes = $\square$ hours	3
9	$60 \div 8 = \square$ r $\square$	7 r 4
10	$49 - 7 - 7 = \square \times 5$	7

B

	Question	Answer
1	How many days in 7 weeks?	49
2	What is four squared divided by 2?	8
3	What is seven-eighths of 16m?	14m
4	Apples cost 9p each. How much will 7 cost?	63p
5	How many times longer is 48km than 8km?	6
6	What is the product of 9 and 12?	108
7	How many whole ones are equal to 42 sixths?	7
8	How many sixes are there in thirty?	5
9	Multiply 2 squared by 3.	12
10	How much greater is (4×5) than (3×4)?	8

C

	Question	Answer
1	A square has sides of 10cm. What is its area?	$100cm^2$
2	Three 60° angles are joined together to make one angle. How large is it?	180°
3	Three in every 5 sweets in a bag are orange. Twenty-one sweets are orange. How many sweets are there altogether in the bag?	35
4	An author writes 4 pages in 3 hours. At this rate how long will it take him to write 24 pages?	18 hr
5	Subtract the product of six and six from the product of ten and ten.	64
6	Write the missing number. $9 \times \square = 60 + 12$	8
7	How many pencils can be bought for £8.10 if a packet of 8 pencils costs 90p?	72
8	To $\frac{2}{3}$ of 24p, add $\frac{4}{5}$ of 30p.	40p
9	The distance from Anby to Ugby is four-fifths of the distance from Anby to Wells. How far is it from Anby to Wells via Ugby?	35km
10	3600ml of oil fill 6 identical containers. How much does each hold?	600ml

Anby
28km
Ugby
Wells

A		Answer
1	$360° \div 4 =$	90°
2	$\frac{5}{6}$ of 42kg is	35kg
3	£80 + £80 + £80 + £80 =	£320
4	$3 \times \square = 2100$	700
5	$(56 \div 7) \times 3 =$	24
6	$9 \times 9 \times 3 \times 0 =$	0
7	$\frac{7}{10}$ of 700mm is	490mm
8	400g × 4 =	1600g
9	$\square \div 9 = 100$	900
10	$3^2 \times 2^2 =$	36

B		Answer
1	What is the product of 80 and 60?	4800
2	How many times longer is 720km than 8km?	90
3	How many groups of 30p are there in £2.70?	9
4	What is 40 times 5 times 90?	18 000
5	Find the total mass of 5 parcels of 600g in kg.	3kg
6	Divide 4 squared by 8.	2
7	What must 6m be multiplied by to give 540m?	90
8	What is (45 ÷ 9) minus (28 ÷ 7)?	1
9	Divide £640 by 8.	£80
10	Find the difference between 7 × 8 and 6 × 11.	10

C		Answer
1	Sixty-three children are grouped in teams of 9. How many teams?	7
2	What number, when multiplied by 9, will give a product that is half of 90?	5
3	A prize of £8100 is shared equally between 9 people. How much money will they each receive?	£900
4	This line is 36mm long. How many millimetres is a line that is $\frac{5}{9}$ of its length?	20mm
5	Divide the square of 20 by 10.	40
6	(30cm) What is the perimeter of this equilateral triangle?	90cm
7	Which of these numbers will divide into 42 without a remainder? 4 6 8 9	6
8	A small bag of sugar holds 400g. How many of these bags do you need to have 2.8kg of sugar?	7
9	The angles in this diagram are equal. What is the size of angle *x*?	45°
10	Nine pieces of ribbon, each 9cm in length, are cut from a metre length. How much ribbon is left?	19cm

A

		Answer
1	$0.5 \times \square = 4.5$	9
2	$11 \times 7 =$	77
3	$4^2 + 2^2 =$	20
4	Three thirteens are	39
5	$0.9 \times \square = 5.4$	6
6	$\square \div 5 = 5$	25
7	$22 \div 11 =$	2
8	$\frac{3}{7}$ of 42cm is	18cm
9	$8\overline{)64}$	8
10	$(5 \times 12) - (6 \times 10) =$	0

B

		Answer
1	What are eight groups of 9?	72
2	What is the area of a square with sides of 7cm?	49cm²
3	Share £3.60 equally among 9 boys. How much each?	40p
4	Find the remainder when 40 is divided by 6.	4
5	Divide 4.8 by 6.	0.8
6	What is the product of 0.7 and 4?	2.8
7	What is $\frac{7}{8}$ of 24?	21
8	How many times smaller is 3 than 33?	11
9	What is 0.3kg multiplied by 9?	2.7kg
10	How many months are there in 6 years?	72

C

		Answer
1	Six pieces of ribbon are cut, each 0.4m in length. What is their total length?	2.4m
2	Find the difference between (0.4×5) and $(1.2 \div 0.3)$.	2
3	A scale drawing shows lengths 9 times smaller than in real life. How long, in real life, is a length that is 0.9cm on the drawing?	8.1cm
4	How long will it take to travel a distance of 63km travelling at 9km/h?	7 hr
5	What is the mean of these 4 numbers? [11 12 5 4]	8
6	A rectangle is 7cm long and 0.8cm wide. What is its area?	5.6cm²
7	The area of a rectangle is 2400cm². If its length is 60cm, what is its width?	40cm
8	If it costs £0.50 to travel 5km, how much will it cost to travel 45km at the same rate?	£4.50
9	What is the perimeter of a regular decagon with sides of 0.06m?	0.6m
10	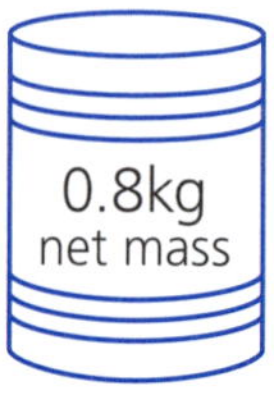 How many grams more than 3kg is the mass of the contents of 4 of these tins?	200g

A		Answer
1	(80 × 30) ÷ 400 =	6
2	11 × 12 =	132
3	☐ ÷ 12 = 2	24
4	$\frac{7}{9}$ of £54 is	£42
5	6 × 8 = ☐ × 12	4
6	☐ × 8 = 5.6	0.7
7	4 × 0.7km =	2.8km
8	The square of 7cm is	49cm^2
9	40 ÷ 9 = ☐ r ☐	4 r 4
10	2 × 3 × 2 × 5 × 2 =	120

B		Answer
1	What is the product of 11 and 8?	88
2	How many lots of 0.6 are in 3.6?	6
3	What is one-seventh of 3.5?	0.5
4	What is the difference between (0.4 × 8) and (0.8 × 4)?	0
5	Find the sum of (9 × 0.3) and (3 × 1.1).	6
6	Share £5.60 equally among 7 boys. How much each?	80p
7	Divide 84 by 7.	12
8	Thirty-two tenths is how many lots of 0.8?	4
9	6 times 2 times 6 is	72
10	What is the remainder when 70 is divided by 8?	6

C		Answer
1	A piece of string 4.8m long is cut into 8 equal pieces. What is the length of one piece?	60cm
2	A bucket holds 8.1 litres of water, which is shared equally between 9 people. How many millilitres of water will they each get?	900ml
3	Eight biscuits cost 72p. How much do seven of the biscuits cost?	63p
4	Three large floor tiles are placed side by side touching in a line. What is their total length? (0.6m, 0.6m, 0.6m)	1.8m
5	Which of these numbers can be divided by both 5 and 12 without a remainder? 10 12 20 24 30 50 60 72	60
6	Chloe has £12. Shappi has seven times as much as that. Find the total of their money.	£96
7	A line is split into parts in the ratio of 4:7. If the line is 55cm long, what are the lengths of the two parts?	20cm 35cm
8	The mean of 4 numbers is 0.4. Three of the numbers are 0.1, 0.8, 0.3. What is the fourth number?	0.4
9	2.1 litres of oil fill 7 identical cups. How much does each hold?	300ml
10	What is the perimeter of a regular dodecagon with sides of 3cm?	36cm

SECTION 2 | Test 9

A

		Answer
1	$4\overline{)3.2}$	0.8
2	9 × 13 =	117
3	$\frac{3}{4}$ of 360° is	270°
4	9 × 8 × 2 × 0 =	0
5	12p + 12p + 12p + 12p =	48p
6	5.4kg ÷ 9 =	0.6kg
7	5.6 ÷ 0.8 =	7
8	0.6 × □ = 0.9 × 4	6
9	29 ÷ 5 = □ r □	5 r 4
10	4 × □ = £2.80	70p

B

		Answer
1	How many minutes are there in 8 hours?	480
2	What is one seventh of 42cm?	6cm
3	12 squared subtract 10 squared is	44
4	What is the product of 8 and 0.9?	7.2
5	How many months are there in 9 years?	108
6	Add (11 × 10) to (5 × 8) and divide by 3.	50
7	How many times heavier is 3.6kg than 1.2kg?	3
8	What number is equal to $8^2 + 4^2$?	80
9	Bananas cost 12p each. How much will 8 cost?	96p
10	Divide 68 by 11.	6 r 2

C

		Answer
1	Four notebooks cost £2.40. What will be the cost of 9 notebooks?	£5.40
2	One-ninth of a number is 0.3. What is the number?	2.7
3	Write the missing number. 9 × 9 = 11 × 8 − □	7
4	What is the smallest number that can be divided by both 12 and 9 without a remainder?	36
5	What is the perimeter of an equilateral triangle with sides of 0.6cm?	1.8cm
6	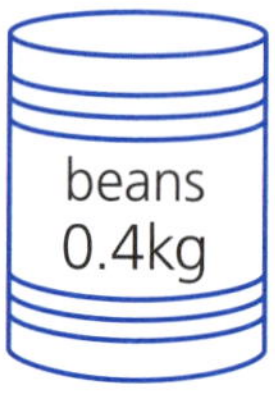 A tin contains 0.4kg of baked beans. Hamed eats $\frac{1}{10}$ of the beans. What mass of beans does he eat?	0.04kg
7	A motorcyclist travels at 36km per hour. How far does he ride in 10 minutes?	6km
8	What is the mean of these 7 numbers? 10 15 6 19 2 5 6	9
9	Seven kg cost £4.90. Find the price per kg.	70p
10	A square mosaic tile has an area of $12cm^2$. Six tiles are used to make a shape, without gaps. What is the area of the shape?	$72cm^2$

SECTION 2 | Test 10

A

		Answer
1	$\frac{2}{3}$ of 360° is	240°
2	100 ÷ 11 = ☐ r ☐	9 r 1
3	$(1^2 + 3^2) \times 7 =$	70
4	3.5 ÷ 5 =	0.7
5	$12\overline{)60}$	5
6	0.8 × ☐ = 3.2	4
7	0.7 × 0.9 =	0.63
8	$\frac{4}{9}$ of 36cm is	16cm
9	(3 × 4) × (2 × 5) × 6 =	720
10	The square of 13cm is	$169cm^2$

B

		Answer
1	Split 42 in the ratio of 3:4.	18 24
2	How many days in 12 weeks?	84
3	Multiply 8 by 0.9.	7.2
4	What is the total mass of 6 sets of 0.8kg?	4.8kg
5	Divide 6.4 by 8.	0.8
6	What are three groups of 0.7?	2.1
7	There are eighty-one ninths. How many whole ones is that?	9
8	How many months are in 11 years?	132
9	What is the product of 7 and 0.8?	5.6
10	How many hours is 540 minutes?	9

C

		Answer
1	● stands for a missing sign, +, −, × or ÷. 1.2 × 6 = 8 ● 0.8 What is the correct sign?	−
2	The radius of the circle is 8cm. What is the length of the diagonal of the square?	16cm
3	How many 9-litre cans can be filled from 63 litres of oil?	7
4	Sana has £11. Ellie has 12 times as much as that. Find the total of their money.	£143
5	Divide the total of 6.9 and 0.8 by 7.	1.1
6	Which of these numbers will divide into 108 without a remainder? 7 8 9 10 11	9
7	This sector of a pie chart is one twelfth of the circle. What is the angle at the centre of the sector?	30°
8	A chocolate bar costs £0.70. How much change from £5 would you get if you bought 7 chocolate bars?	10p
9	What is one-sixth of the product of 8 and 9?	12
10	A rectangle has an area of $2.8cm^2$. Its width is 0.7cm. What is its length?	4cm

A — Answer

1. 4 × 0.7kg = 2.8kg
2. (0.4 ÷ 5) × (6 × 0) = 0
3. 4.8 ÷ 1.2 = 4
4. $\square^2$ = 64 — 8
5. 7.2 ÷ 9 = 0.8
6. (6 × 2) × ☐ = 84 — 7
7. ☐ ÷ 11 = 11 — 121
8. 0.9m + 0.9m + 0.9m = 2.7m
9. $\frac{3}{7}$ of 49m is 21m
10. ☐ hours = 300 minutes — 5

B — Answer

1. Find the mean of 12, 9, 10, 17. — 12
2. How much greater is 9 squared than 1 squared? — 80
3. What is one-sixth of 2.4km? — 0.4km
4. What number is equal to 0.8 times 6? — 4.8
5. What is the product of 4 and 13? — 52
6. How many times smaller is 70 than 350? — 5
7. Multiply (4 × 3) by 9. — 108
8. Share £5.40 equally between 6 boys. How much each? — 90p
9. How many quarters in 8? — 32
10. How many months are there in 12 years? — 144

C — Answer

1. When a number is divided by 3 the answer is 12. What is the number? — 36
2. Cho gave 5 friends 12 sweets each and she had 9 sweets left. How many did she have to start with? — 69
3. One-seventh of a number is 8. What is the number? — 56
4. £96 is shared between Li and Sandeep. Li gets 7 times as much as Sandeep. How much does Li get? — £84
5. Eight identical tins have a total mass of 5.6kg. What is the mass of 6 of the tins? — 4.2kg
6. What is the total cost of 7 books and 3 pencil cases? — £84

   book £9

   pencil case £7

7. A van can travel 9km using one litre of petrol. How far can it travel using 0.9 litres? — 8.1km
8. This line is 6cm long. Another is 1.2 times longer. What is its length? — 7.2cm
9. What is the difference between the number of days in 11 weeks and the months in 6 years? — 5
10. What is the mean of these 8 numbers?

1	0.5	0.5	0.2	0.2	0.2	0.3	0.3

   0.4

SECTION 2 | Test 12

A	Answer
1 $\frac{8}{9}$ of 4.5kg is	4kg
2 1 × 1 × 1 × 1 × 1 × 1 =	1
3 ▢^{2} = 121	11
4 £1.20 + £1.20 + £1.20 + £1.20 =	£4.80
5 99 ÷ 9 = ▢ ÷ 12	132
6 6.3 ÷ 0.7 =	9
7 (6 × 2) × (4 × 3) =	144
8 6^2 ÷ 9 =	4
9 $\frac{5}{9}$ of 180° is	100°
10 ▢ ÷ 13 = 6	78

B	Answer
1 Twice 12 = 3 times ▢	8
2 Split 56 in the ratio of 3:4.	24 32
3 What is the product of 0.6 and 7?	4.2
4 How many times heavier is 2.8kg than 0.4kg?	7
5 Divide 2.4 by 4.	0.6
6 How many months are there in 8 years?	96
7 There are twenty-five fifths. How many whole ones is that?	5
8 What is 7 squared plus 3 squared?	58
9 Which number, other than 1, 2, 3, 4, 6, 12 and 24, divides exactly into 24?	8
10 By how much is $\frac{5}{8}$ of 48 greater than $\frac{8}{9}$ of 27?	6

C	Answer
1 Eighty-four chairs are arranged in rows of 12. How many rows?	7
2 On a clock-face, what is the angle between the hands when the time is 1 o'clock?	30°
3 A pencil costs £0.60 and a paintbrush costs £1.20. How much will it cost in total to buy 3 pencils and 5 paintbrushes?	£7.80
4 What number, when multiplied by 5, will give a product of 2.0?	0.4
5 Divide the total of 1.7 and 0.4 by 3.	0.7
6 The angles in this diagram are equal. What is the size of angle x?	120°
7 A line is split into parts in the ratio of 3:8. If the line is 88cm long, what are the lengths of the two parts?	24cm 64cm
8 The mean of 6 numbers is 9. Five of the numbers are 5 5 10 10 20. What is the sixth number?	4
9 What is the perimeter of a regular nonagon with sides of 0.9cm?	8.1cm
10 The radius of the circle is 9cm. What is the length of the diagonal of the square?	18cm

PROGRESS TEST 2

Write the numbers 1 to 20 down the side of a sheet of paper.
Write alongside these numbers the **answers only** to the following questions.
Work as quickly as you can. Time allowed – **10 minutes**.

1 40g × 13 = — 520g

2 What is $\frac{3}{7}$ of 28? — 12

3 60 ÷ 9 = ☐ r ☐ — 6 r 6

4 $☐^2 = 49$ — 7

5 What is the product of 0.6 and 7? — 4.2

6 How long will it take to travel a distance of 36km travelling at 4km/h? — 9 hr

7 80 × 3 = 4 × ☐ — 60

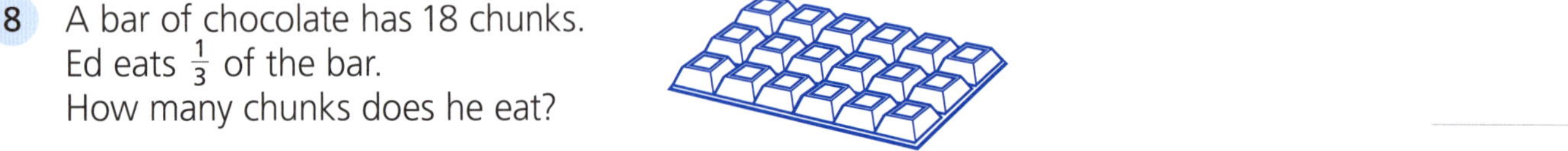

8 A bar of chocolate has 18 chunks.
Ed eats $\frac{1}{3}$ of the bar.
How many chunks does he eat? — 6

9 Split £56 in the ratio of 3:5. — £21 £35

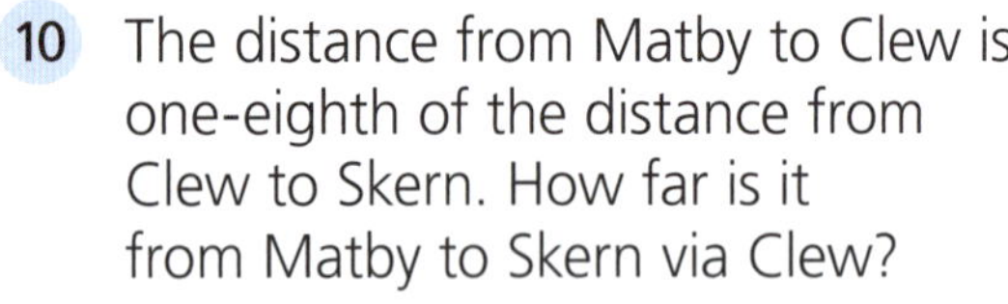

10 The distance from Matby to Clew is one-eighth of the distance from Clew to Skern. How far is it from Matby to Skern via Clew? — 7.2km

11 What is 12 squared subtract 6 squared? — 108

12 What is the remainder when 111 is divided by 11? — 1

13 The mean of 6 numbers is 8. Five of the numbers are 5 5 10 10 15
What is the sixth number? — 3

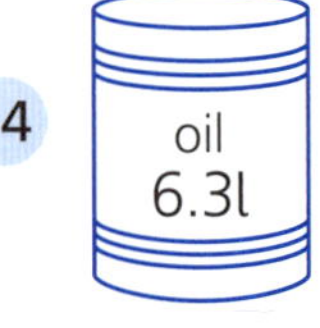

14 A tin contains 6.3 litres of oil. Simon uses one-seventh of the oil.
How much is left? — 5.4l

15 What is the difference between (0.9 × 9) and (1.1 × 11)? — 4

16 A bucket holds 8.4 litres of water, which is shared equally between 7 people.
How many millilitres of water will they each get? — 1200ml

17 Nine bricks have a mass of 2.7kg. How many bricks have a mass of 3.6kg? — 12

18 The perimeter of a square is 160mm. What is its area in square millimetres? — $1600mm^2$

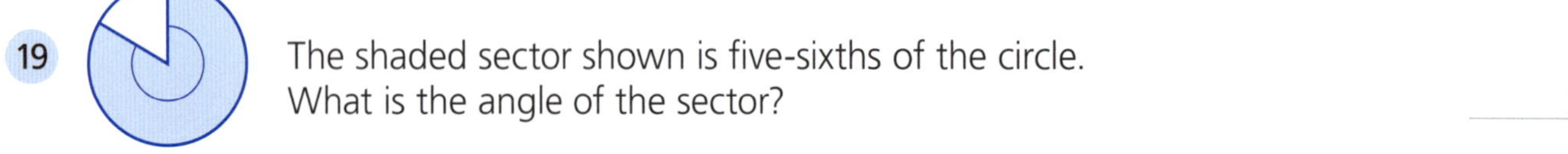

19 The shaded sector shown is five-sixths of the circle.
What is the angle of the sector? — 300°

20 Divide the difference between 10^2 and 2^2 by 12. — 8

PROGRESS TEST 2 | Group record sheet

The **Group record sheet** can be used to record the pupils' scores each time they attempt **Progress test 2**.

Class/Set	Teacher's name

Pupil's name	1st attempt	2nd attempt	3rd attempt	4th attempt

Multiplication facts cards: questions

2 × 2	4 × 8	7 × 7	10 × 10
2 × 5	4 × 10	7 × 8	10 × 11
2 × 12	5 × 5	7 × 12	10 × 12
3 × 3	5 × 6	8 × 2	11 × 6
3 × 7	5 × 11	8 × 3	11 × 7
3 × 9	6 × 2	9 × 5	12 × 3
4 × 4	6 × 9	9 × 7	12 × 4
4 × 6	6 × 10	9 × 8	12 × 12

Multiplication facts cards: answers

4	32	49	100
10	40	56	110
24	25	84	120
9	30	16	66
21	55	24	77
27	12	45	36
16	54	63	48
24	60	72	144

GLOSSARY

Here is a list of the mathematical vocabulary used in **Times Tables Tests 1** and **2**.

area	the amount of surface space inside the perimeter of a shape – area is often measured in square centimetres (cm^2) or square metres (m^2)
consecutive	consecutive numbers follow each other in order – 1, 2, 3, 4 are consecutive, as are 11, 12, 13, 14
difference	the difference between two numbers is the answer to one number take away another number – the difference between 10 and 4 is the same as 10 take away 4
divide	to split things into equal groups – you can divide 8 into 2 equal groups with 4 in each (8 ÷ 2 = 4 or divide 8 by 2 = 4)
double	when you double something you make it twice as big – doubling is the same as multiplying by 2, so double 8 is 16 because 8 × 2 = 16
equilateral	an equilateral triangle is a triangle which has sides that are all the same length and angles that are the same measurement
fraction	divide something into equal parts and each part is called a fraction
halve	divide something into two equal parts and it has been halved
mean	the sum of a group of numbers divided by the number of numbers in that group – the mean of 2, 3 and 4 is 2 + 3 + 4 divided by 3
multiple	the multiple of a number can be divided exactly by that number – 4, 6, 8 and 200 are all multiples of 2 because they can be divided by 2 with no remainder
multiply	to times one number by another – 4 × 8 means '4 multiplied by 8' or '4 times 8' ('multiply 4 by 8')
perimeter	the perimeter of a shape is the total measurement of all its sides
product	the product of two numbers is the same as multiplying them – the product of 3 and 7 is the same as 3 × 7
radius	the distance from the centre of a circle to the edge
remainder	the number left over when a number cannot be divided equally by another number – 12 divided by 10 is 1 with a remainder of 2, or 1 r 2
share	another way of dividing ('share 12 coins between 4 people')
squared	a number that is squared is multiplied by itself – 3 squared is written as '3^2', which is 3 × 3
sum	the sum of two or more numbers is the same as adding them – the sum of 2 and 2 is the same as 2 + 2
times	can mean 'multiplied by' – 6 times 2 is 12 or 6 × 2 = 12
a whole	something that is not divided into parts